Literature for Democracy

Literature for Democracy
Reading as a Social Act

Gordon M. Pradl

Boynton/Cook Publishers
Heinemann
Portsmouth, NH

Boynton/Cook Publishers, Inc.
A subsidiary of Reed Elsevier Inc.
361 Hanover Street
Portsmouth, NH 03801–3912

Offices and agents throughout the world

We would like to thank those who have given their permission to include material in this book.

"Coming down the Kuskokwim" by Peter R. Stillman was originally published in *College English* (55, 2, February 1993). Reprinted by permission of the author and publisher.

Excerpts from YOU CAN'T SAY YOU CAN'T PLAY by Vivian Paley. Copyright © 1992 by the President and Fellows of Harvard College. Reprinted by permission of the publisher, Harvard University Press, Cambridge, Mass.

Excerpts from LITERATURE AS EXPLORATION by Louise Rosenblatt. Copyright © 1938, 1968. Published by Noble and Noble. Reprinted by permission of the author.

"Grandmother's Ring" by Kathleen Jamie was originally published in ISLAND OF THE CHILDREN: AN ANTHOLOGY OF NEW POEMS, edited by Angela Huth. Copyright © 1987. Published by Orchard Books, London. Reprinted by permission of the author.

"First Gestures" by Julia Kasdorf was originally published in *Poetry* (165, 5, February 1995). Reprinted by permission of the Editor of *Poetry*.

Library of Congress Cataloging-in-Publication Data
Pradl, Gordon M.
   Literature for democracy : reading as a social act / Gordon M. Pradl.
      p. cm.
   Includes bibliographical references and index.
   ISBN 0-86709-380-3 (alk. paper)
    1. Literature—Study and teaching—Social aspects. 2. Reading—Social aspects. 3. Reader-response criticism. I. Title.
   LB1575.P73   1996
   372.64–dc20   95–47260
                                                   CIP

Editor: Peter Stillman
Cover design: Philip Augusta
Manufacturing: Louise Richardson

Printed in the United States of America on acid-free paper
99 98 97 96 DA 1 2 3 4 5 6

Contents

Preface
ix

One
Desiring Democracy
1

Two
Surviving in the Hall of Mirrors
12

Three
Challenging Authority in the Classroom
23

Four
Students Speaking Up for Themselves
34

Five
Rethinking Our Privilege and Status
41

Six
Listening to Ourselves
51

Seven
The World from Another Perspective
58

Eight
The Teacher as Listener
66

Nine
Literature and Exploration
74

Ten
The Impasse of Reader Response
81

Eleven
Entering the Dance of Conversation
94

Twelve
Conversational Responses to Poems
107

Thirteen
Conversing About Literature Without a Teacher
120

Fourteen
A Democracy of Readers and Readings
131

Fifteen
Invitations and Possibilities
146

Works Cited
153

Index
159

In memory of my father
George Pradl

and my uncles
Gordon Morrell
Douglas Morrell
Donald Morrell

Preface

In this book I ask the question, What does democracy have to do with the reading and teaching of literature?

My answer: *reading is a social act.* This view acknowledges a natural tension between individual and group as we go about the difficult work of developing democratic relationships. Initially, a person must be able to assert with confidence his or her own individuality, but such assertions necessarily encounter the perspectives (and desires) of others. Consequently, our responses to the world and its texts inevitably embroil us in social controversy. Living with others democratically involves endless conflicts and contradictions as we try to resist hierarchical arrangements. Yet, because we welcome the complications of alternative realities—value pluralism, we commit ourselves to dialogue and negotiation as a means of including voices that are not our own.

In our literature classes, as we talk with students about the poems we read together, we share an important opportunity to learn about and practice democracy. The literary text, because of its characteristic openness and indeterminacy, invites each reader to enter a *transaction* that yields his or her unique response. But our response is satisfying to us only when we celebrate it and compare it with other responses. By placing our readings in the context of other readings, we begin to participate in a democratic enterprise of negotiated meaning. Being in a democratic relationship with other readers, we begin to appreciate how the individuality of our responses and interpretations can be extended and strengthened as we engage differing points of view. Literature classrooms might be caldrons of democracy, depending on how we, as teachers, enable students to connect with their own readings and with the readings of others.

To begin the process of creating a democratic spirit in our literature classes, we need to reflect on a key paradox of our profession—our *authority* as teachers of literature. For me, questions about a teacher's role and status relate to larger issues of authority with which we constantly struggle in our democracy. Autonomy and personal freedom are not always commensurate with the needs of community, and our teaching authority often prevents us from recognizing the ways we hold back students from gaining their own independence. To focus these concerns, I explore my reading of a short story—one that has resonated for me around the issue of authority throughout my years of teaching. This experience allows me to suggest that an individual's response to a text exists most vitally in conversation with the responses of others. With this in mind, I argue that, as teachers, our democratic responsibility is to approach poems and stories in a manner that invites students into the conversation, rather than dominates or condemns their less-experienced reading responses.

Integral to negotiating our meanings with students is the power of the empathic attention we give them through *listening*. I see listening as the social process central to democratic experience. If we are to encourage students to begin with their own literary responses, then as teachers we must be prepared to hear them. We are not just listening until we hear the "right" answer! Because listening validates students' perceptions, it shifts the patterns of social control in the classroom. It raises questions: Who gets to talk? Whose words are valuable enough to be heard? By attending to students, we legitimize a democracy of voices. As teachers, however, we also need to be heard. This keeps us connected to our own stories and how they relate to our reading responses—a fundamental prerequisite if our listening presence in the classroom is to elicit and take seriously the stories and responses of the students.

More than thirty years before the rise of reader-response theory, Louise Rosenblatt pioneered the idea of literature as an experiential *transaction* among self, text, and other readers. In doing this, she helped establish the social bearings for our democratic conversations with and about poems. By emphasizing the important dynamic of each reader's response, Rosenblatt shows us how emotion and reason form an essential partnership when we read works of literature. As we begin to appreciate the full scope of Rosenblatt's social agenda, we see how it challenges all authoritarian approaches to teaching literature.

Finally, you will see that I focus on the role of conversation in social reading. In particular, I emphasize that each reader has a unique reading history that must be taken into account as we encourage sharing and negotiation. Also, I offer two extended examples of a procedure—written conversation—that intensifies the process of social reading by slowing it down so that we may better listen to each other.

Writing the numerous drafts of this book has provided me with an important opportunity to reflect on my own teaching. I have come to see that our relationships with others (how we organize ourselves socially) intimately influences our reading of literature, both our reading theories and our reading practices. It is easy to spout progressive, democratic ideas; it is much harder to enact them in concrete situations. By telling some of the stories of my own teaching and learning experiences, of my own encounters with students, I've learned to appreciate how easy it is for me to be trapped by hierarchical habits of teaching literature. Such reflection has proved liberating, and I hope the personal side of this book will encourage other teachers of literature to consider the stories of their own practices in relation to the goals and theories they find themselves espousing. Together, in wider circles of reflection and conversation, let us convene democratic classrooms in which students come to know the power and pleasure of their individual and social readings.

The composing of this book benefited from constant dialogue with colleagues and students: John Mayher, Marilyn Sobelman, Harold Vine, John Rouse, Louise Rosenblatt, Barbara Danish, Nancy Lester, Joy Boyum, Mitchell Leaska, Margot Ely, Marlene Barron, Peter Stillman, Jimmy Britton, Nancy Martin, Jenifer Smith, Mike Simmons, Mike Hayhoe, Patrick Dias, Myra Barrs, Tony Haynes, Darlene Forrest, Julia Kasdorf, Jane Douglas, Mary K. Healy, Rosemary Howard, Marion Mumford, Jeff Finlay, Andy Weitz, Alfie Guy, Heather Masri, George Bain, Gigi Jasper, and the group of young women in Stradbroke who helped launch the "written conversations." Each of you, in your own manner, encourages me to see the text as an invitation for democratic conversation. And finally, my thanks to Mary Ann, who is always there with patience and love.

Chapter One

Desiring Democracy

Who do I wish to become? Even as we mouth these words, the ideas of *becoming* and *self-determination* bang up against sobering realities beyond our control. At birth, each of us is ensnared in a particular social ethic, constrained by a particular social horizon. Indeed, few social arrangements or beliefs even allow people to know *wishes* of becoming or of selfhood in the first place.

Stories of possibility and of change risk dislocating a person's relationship to authority and the certainty granted by its order and orientation. And so throughout history, those in dominant cultural positions have silenced narratives of transformation constructed by their "inferiors." Imagining and asserting one's own agency necessarily disturbs the interests of some hierarchy already in place.

Democracy, however, insists on a new line of vision. Democracy awakens our potential to hold dominion over our own lives. It suggests that each of us owns a unique perspective that others are bound to honor. But, in unleashing the promise of the *individual*, democracy also uncovered its characteristic social dilemma: How might we learn to recognize and respect the perspectives of others without betraying our own interests?

It is, of course, too simple to say that one important answer to this democratic dilemma might originate in the consciousness that is provoked when two or more people come together to share the multiple meanings they've made of a *poem*. Still, imagine that as a possibility.

1

Coming Down the Kuskokwim

Last night I saw a pair
of swans lift from the water
and fly wingtip to wingtip
along the thin sky. If
I say they were as pure
in the air as early love—
if I say my spirit rose
with them—you would say yes,
for we have sat five days
in the same circle. We
are alive in each other.

The river flowed silent as
a wish toward a single star.
A dozen swallows bloomed
above it. A friend had told
me they are sacred. If he killed
one, he would have to bury it
and say a prayer. We fished
the same stream side by side;
when we stood at the edge
of a pond, our reflections fell
within its circle. So I said yes.
Now we are alive in each other.

                    —Peter Stillman

Germaine, Robin, Whitney, Leslie, and Morgan gather to talk
about Peter's poem. After reading it aloud to the group several
times, Morgan offers a response, "Ah, a love poem. It makes me feel
contented—swans graceful in their passage across the sky, two people mirrored in unison, reflected in a spiritual circle of water. Rest-
ful, peaceful. The word *alive* for me evokes a sense of calm, of inner
harmony. I like to imagine life being more than a jumbled, frenetic
rat race. With those swans, and the river, and the lovers, suddenly
I'm back with 'The Wild Swans at Coole.' Where is the Kuskokwim,
the Kusk-aw-kwim, the Kus-kawk-wim? My mind drifts slowly back
to nature."

Exploding with impatience, Whitney interrupts this reverie.
"Rubbish! Morgan, can't you see the poet working his magic to well
up our sentiments? These aren't genuine tears in our eyes; it's just
another retreat from the real world. Everywhere people are suffering
daily and this guy's privileged enough to be fishing somewhere out
in the wilderness. Come on. It's precisely these fake feelings that
give poetry a bad name. Now, if we read this poem in a history or a

sociology class, we'd get the real picture. Next this poet'll be leading us into some kind of occult trance, being at one with nature or
being reborn with his medicine man friend."

Robin intervenes, slightly exasperated. "You two always argue
this way, but I'm not sure where it gets us. Must we reduce everything to love and nature versus economics and politics? Can't we
agree to suspend judgment a moment and just ask some questions?
Yes, the poem made me feel good, but it's really quite slippery.
Who's in love with whom? I see one of those doubling gestalt figures in my mind's eye. You know, old hag/beautiful woman or rab-
bit/duck. It's moving in and out between love for the opposite sex
and love for the same sex. Peter is a man, and thus I presume he's
the 'I' of the poem, so I'd want to know: Is this a seduction lament
or an affirmation of male bonding? I can just feel what you're going
to say, but it drives me crazy having to hold both these interpretations in suspension at once. If Peter were here, his simple intention
might clear up the ambiguity."

Silently pondering the conversation so far, Germaine at last enters the speaker's circle. "Now that I read it again, after what the
three of you've said, I suddenly see that the poem calls for a political interpretation. Everything depends on what's not said directly.
We must look at the margins. The poet's making a plea for the unity
of world peace—'a wish toward a single star.' If only people would
stop warring against each other, then we might all come within the
same circle."

Leslie, however, will have nothing to do with Germaine's sup-
positions. "I don't believe I'm hearing this. A political reading is
both too easy and outrageous. I will acknowledge that this is a
cross-cultural poem. If the poet belonged naturally in this wilderness, he wouldn't be making a point of the restriction against shoot-
ing swallows. So a kind of bridging is occurring. I see the poet
connecting with someone in another culture, but more than that—
another time and space within the sweep of history, as though the
20th century was fleeing back to an earlier, more coherent order."

Meanwhile, Whitney can barely stay contained, wanting to remain focused on the rights issue. "But what right does this white
man have to intrude on the inner circles of these aboriginal people.
This is a really blind and insensitive, noble-savage poem, and we
need to alert ourselves to our own dangerously narrow, ethnocentric
feelings here."

Then, once again, the mediating voice of Robin tries to encourage a more encompassing perspective. "Doesn't anyone think we
need to take into account the fact that Peter recently spent some

time teaching in Alaska? Perhaps it would help to see the images in the poem in the context of ice and snow. I like the reverberations here, that people exist apart, but deeply need the *other,* need *each other.* The poem feels very personal. And so, while I have to imagine referents for the pronouns, they don't feel obscure. Just as the swallows are sacred, so this poem creates for me a sacred moment of connection, of communion."

And so the five companions continue their dance of response and interpretation.

Feelings, emotions, ideas, perspectives, conjecture, contradiction, argument, mediation, negotiation—the pleasures of staying together in relationships. To read Peter's poem alone is not to get the half of it. When as readers we openly collide with the readings of others, we begin to see beyond our original boundaries. In listening to each other, we discover how much more we might become than if we had remained in isolation. But seeing reading this way—as a social act of becoming—involves committing ourselves to the unique paradoxes of the ongoing democratic experiment. In this experiment, we seek ways of living with each other that encourage openness and tolerance, as difficult as this may be, since our ideal is to value the person, not the particular group or hierarchical status of the person.

The Tensions of Democracy

Everyone will have their own sense of what democracy means, of how it relates to freedom and equality, liberty and justice, rights and responsibilities. However defined, democracy is certain to disturb existing arrangements. In decrying power and privilege, it proposes that most persons are quite capable of determining what is best for themselves. Thus, not surprisingly, elites, regardless of their persuasion, have generally viewed democracy with suspicion, even alarm. The spread of democracy summons the rise of individual autonomy, and there are those who view this as unraveling the very fabric of society.

Many philosophers have scoffed at the people's competence to manage their own affairs. Plato, one of the first to observe the unsettling reality of democratic decision making, concluded that the mass of citizens did not possess the proper understanding to choose either the best rulers or the wisest course of action. Caught in the clutches of pure appetite and self-gratification, the people could not refrain from personal gain or corruption, nor could they aspire to what is truly beautiful and divine. Much later, as democracy gradually replaced oligarchical forms of government in the West, those in power continued to fear progressive developments, convinced that they were witnessing the downfall of civilization itself. Judged from their "superior" vantage point, democracy seemed to promote aimless drift by sanctioning every strata of society to do just what it pleases. Enthroning liberty invited chaos and perhaps even anarchy. Freedom of expression spelled a lapse in coherence and mutual interdependence.

But an even deeper complaint remains: democracy promotes mediocrity and abandons standards. In a democracy, life supposedly descends to the lowest common denominator—everyone comes to resemble everyone else. Much of this thinking, however, represents the defensive posturing of cultural elites. Despising the chaotic and fast-paced life in modern times, George Santayana, the Harvard philosopher, succinctly represented this elitist position almost a century ago when he wondered if people wouldn't find more happiness "in the old aristocratic doctrine that the good is not liberty, but wisdom, and contentment with one's natural restrictions; the classical tradition knew that only a few can win" (Durant, p. 549). The problem, as Santayana saw it, was that democracy initiates "the great free-for-all, catch-as-catch-can wrestling match of laissez-faire industrialism" (p. 549) and, as there is always more for which to compete, people always remain dissatisfied.

Such complaints suggest a rejection of what is perhaps democracy's central characteristic: access. Individuals should be able to exert some control over their own destinies, and, for this to happen, opportunities must be manifest. Indeed, in a democracy, no matter how egregiously this principle may be violated, its hope and energy persists. Democracy invites citizens to see life as self-determined, and democracy waits to record the lives of those who traditionally have remained in obscurity. Everyone is entitled to recount his or her own history and envision his or her own future.

In America, the idea of access, of respect for multiple perspectives, has developed slowly, grudgingly. There has been much to overcome. In The Radicalism of the American Revolution, his study of our long road to democracy, Gordon Wood shows the successive transformations that have occurred in the American world view. Beginning with monarchical traditions—with their emphasis on hierarchy, authoritarianism, and certainty—the American mind could not just magically become democratic. There had to be a gradual social revolution so that endless patterns of subordination might be supplanted by an egalitarianism based on merit. Republicanism served as a transitional stage in which the old ties of thought and association were initially broken. And while our greatest political thinkers, from Thomas Jefferson and James Madison to John Adams and Alexander Hamilton, set the stage for a massive infusion of liberty and self-government, they too remained wedded to systems of privilege and the notion that disinterested elites were all that prevented the mob from plunging society into chaos and anarchy.

Working Toward Democratic Relationships

Perhaps democracy isn't for everyone. But who gets to decide? The point is that democracy never appears spontaneously, naturally. People work toward it and educate for it. Living together in diversity forces us to consider what constitutes our common culture, how we arrive at shared meanings, and what differences need to be mediated. How fragile democracy becomes when we forget the other person, and he or she forgets us. Yet this is a problem we struggle with every day in our democracy. What do we do with individuals and groups who practice beliefs that allow no room for the free existence of their competitors?

Trying to grant a free existence to others in the space that we're also occupying causes much stress. It's more than just suspending aggression and hostility. It requires getting beyond our initial ignorance of the other person. Yet this often changes precisely those conditions that people most fear changing. Committing ourselves to reciprocity and mediation inevitably alters both who we are and who we might become.

Like most, I will never be completely predisposed to democracy; someone is always playing their music too loudly and I go mad. Faced with the demands and adjustments of social living, I often want it all to go away. I want to live in the present, with my bearings fixed and secure. I want to stop worrying about the latest problem waiting to be solved. I don't want to be forever changing. I want an ordered place, knowing where I fit in relation to the next person in the hierarchy. I want to exclude all that is different from what I am and what I know to be true. I get tired of arguing with everyone who disagrees with me. Can't we just do it *my* way? Then democracy whispers in my ear, telling me to be patient or the story of the *other* will be lost.

Yet, even while many individuals clash trying to prove the superiority of their specific group affiliations, there are those citizens who seem comfortable negotiating and staying with the messiness of democracy. They remain centered despite the conflicts and the bad feelings associated with human relationships. Such persons entertain the perspective of the *other* without losing their own volition. By resisting a cultural tendency to pursue one's own selfish interests, such citizens keep striving to bring the outsider inside. They understand that the cult of the individual, however appealing, finally ends by transforming our grievances and complaints into quarrels and estrangements, rather than conversations and reconciliations. For them, self-other reciprocity is the basis for social living.

Democracy, John Dewey said, "is primarily a mode of associated living, of conjoint communicated experience . . . [Citizens] participate in an interest so that each has to refer his own action to that of others, and to consider the action of others to give point and direction to his own . . . [This results in a] breaking down of those barriers of class, race, and national territory [and today we would add *gender*] which kept men [and women] from perceiving the full import of their activity" (Dewey, 1916/1966, p. 87). And, most importantly, Dewey concluded, "since a democratic society repudiates the principle of external authority, it must find a substitute in voluntary disposition and interest; these can be created only by education" (p. 87).

By seeking to replace the static term *interaction* with the concept of *transaction* in the area of human affairs, Dewey highlighted the importance of casting a critical eye on all privileged hierarchies—whether of people, institutions, practices, or ideas. Because democracy is always looking to the future, it depends dynamically on the kind of change against which hierarchies constantly work. Hierarchies prefer control over transformation. In contrast, Dewey was committed to a society in which citizens try to solve the problems of living through the experimental method, without resorting to predetermined and dogmatic structures. Observing that democratic social life is characterized by mutuality and permeation, Dewey showed us that all parties thrive by being in some way altered in the course of cooperative play, dialogue, and work. No participant is the same after a social transaction.

Individuals develop democratically when things are not fixed in advance, but are open to negotiation and mediation. While democracy inspires us to see that all plans begin with separate individuals and their responses and interpretations, quickly one person is conversing with another. Democracy encourages the growth of individual citizens, not to sanction the excesses of liberty—of staying apart in competition—but to set human relationships on a new footing. This new footing represents an attempt to remain engaged with the conflicts and paradoxes of human relationships through stories of negotiation. When the dignity of the individual is valued, freedom should serve to move people together, not apart, as relationships proceed tentatively across previously restricted boundaries. In a democracy, individuals gain a future by creatively imagining spaces for others.

In describing open-mindedness as the keystone of a democratic culture, Jerome Bruner rightly enumerates the precarious checks and balances that a democracy entails. An open quality of mind, Bruner says, constitutes "a willingness to construe knowledge and values from multiple perspectives without loss of commitment to one's own values" (Bruner, p. 30). The promise, however, never obviates the attendant dilemmas:

> We have learned with much pain, that democratic culture is neither divinely ordained nor is it to be taken for granted as perennially durable. Like all cultures, it is premised upon values that generate distinctive ways of life and corresponding conceptions of reality. Though it values the refreshments of surprise, it is not always proof against the shocks that open-mindedness sometimes inflicts. Its very open-mindedness generates its own enemies, for there is surely a biological constraint on appetites for novelty. (p. 30)

Continuing, Bruner sees constructivism as centrally expressing a democratic culture. This is because such an intellectual approach "demands that we be conscious of how we come to our knowledge and as conscious as we can be about the values that lead us to our perspectives" (p. 30). Accountability and responsibility are crucial here, but this does not mean that only one way of constructing meaning is possible. Bruner advocates open-mindedness and its corollary, constructivism, because he sees these values as best able to cope "with the changes and disruptions that have become so much a feature of modern life" (p. 30). Further, this way of relating democratically to one another must constantly be earned and revitalized.

The selfhood that democracy makes possible brings with it a never-ending spiral of problems, contradictions, and paradoxes. For instance, acknowledging our deep-seated propensity for hierarchy, authority, and certainty—our lack of trust in our "inferiors"—reveals the kind of social effort required if we truly desire democracy. As John Burnheim notes in *Is Democracy Possible?,*

> Revolution does not create new relationships. They emerge out of gradual social change, especially the emergence and diffusion of new practices. New practices can be introduced deliberately only when they can be clearly described and taught. Even then they will not endure unless they become interwoven with the fabric of social practices and social motivations. (Burnheim, p. 155)

Thus, when we come to consider the kinds of talk about literature that might happen in school, it will be important to consider the patterns of exchange that are enacted and how self-determination is encouraged for individual readers, even as they are testing their responses and interpretations on each other. If the tensions of democracy are not openly on display in the literature classroom, students will continue to learn that their meanings are more properly controlled by others.

Reading and Democracy

Textual interpretation lies at the heart of democratic relationships—the creation and mediation of a rich cacophony of narratives. Forms of literature, from canonical tomes to back-fence gossip, have always constituted both group and personal identity in the world. Democracy, however, alters one's approaches to literary texts. Reversed is the ancient stance of blind reverence. Thus, in important aspects, democratic readers begin addressing texts with a new sense of critical and interpretive responsibility. Indeed, it's a quite recent development, historically, for people to admit openly that a *personal* connection may exist between them and the texts they are reading, let alone that this may have consequences for the social scheme of things.

If people in a democracy are to reach their full potential, then they must not defeat themselves in advance. Unfortunately, schooling in numerous ways sends quite undemocratic messages about who can soar and who must remain grounded—not everyone is allowed to become who they wish. Therefore, when we as teachers commit ourselves to democratic relationships, we must seek to create protective, mutual spaces where self-expression may grow. When students' responses are respected by teachers in a democratic setting, they develop confidence in voicing their thoughts. The path to individual agency, to self-determination, inevitably involves social testing. Thus self-expression is never merely idiosyncratic. Whether in harmony or dissonance, self-expression derives from a democratic procession of voices. Having questioned traditional hierarchical arrangements in society, democracy allows a new kind of social dialogue to supersede accidents of birth as the means to self-fulfillment.

Sharing literary readings can inspire democratic satisfaction. In a democracy, literary response is not a search for final meaning. Rather, democracy promotes the collaborative mediation necessary for readers to share and evolve their interpretations. Each new poem—just as each new person—has the potential for speaking to our imagination and defining anew some understanding we have of the world. Thus, all imaginative literature can be seen as challenging or rearranging our preconceived notions. To begin with, there exists a certain amount of common ground in the texts we're reading, enough so that we can talk with others and be understood. At this point, if we are willing, we join as active participants in a conversation composed of many voices, but no final word. As we attune ourselves to these reading exchanges, our social selves continue to evolve.

Democratic enterprises begin with citizens having the convictions of their own responses. Everyone begins with his or her own initial construction of the poem. Yet as individual readings emerge, readers understand the importance of remaining open to conflicting points of view. The alternative is to slip back into the isolated venues of one's original responses. Openness requires constant negoti ation so that the reader respects both individual diversity and group solidarity. By emphasizing reading as a *social activity,* we stay alert to how important the interpersonal is to our understanding and appreciation of texts.

In undemocratic classrooms, driven as they tend to be by facts and tests, reading poems or novels is often reduced to the mere transfer of information. In contrast, democratic teaching fosters multifaceted readings, and discussions are built on layers of agreement and disagreement. Literature education that promotes transformation always entails some significant change in perspective. How consequential this can be is persuasively underscored by Toni Morrison's commentary on slave narratives:

> The prohibition against teaching a slave to read and write (which in many Southern states carried severe punishment) and against a slave's learning to read and write had to be scuttled at all costs. These writers knew that literacy was power. Voting, after all, was inextricably connected to the ability to read; literacy was a way of assuming and proving the "humanity" that the Constitution denied them. That is why the narratives carry the subtitle "written by himself," or "herself," and include introductions and prefaces by white sympathizers to authenticate them. . . . A literate slave was supposed to be a contradiction in terms. (Morrison, pp. 107–108)

When a mind collides with a text in open conversation, prepare for the unexpected. Often, students will take off in directions I had not anticipated as teacher and this threatens my control. If a student rejects the interpretation of the text being featured in my "lesson" and instead invents a new one, both the previous interpretation and the authority that had precariously sustained it become open to question. Given that all hypotheses and beliefs need exposure to criticism in a democracy (implying they might eventually fail and have to be replaced), we might imagine every literature classroom littered with collapsing textual interpretations, where earlier readings are resisted by the next gathering of readers.

In the midst of these alternate readings, I stand nervously as teacher, sometimes on the "wrong" side of the interpretation. With traditions to keep, and hierarchies to uphold before I sleep, I would certainly find it easier to back away from these endless reversals. This highlights my struggle with teaching literature: How can I contain my monologic tendencies and not disrupt the pluralistic conversation of response and interpretation that furthers the values of democracy? Teaching involves staying with the mess that is democracy, rather than being seduced by the efficiencies of unquestioned authority.

In exploring how reading literature as a social act contributes to democratic relationships, I find it important to keep my own story constantly in mind. I can't just make pronouncements about democracy for others without considering my own contradictions and reversals. Often, I remain unaware of how I too resist democracy. Thus, the explorations on the pages that follow are my attempt to understand the dilemmas I've faced as a teacher of English and to explain why I have struggled with the problems of access, perspective, and confidence.

Democratic teaching and learning, despite its difficulties, releases the widest range of possibilities in the social individual. By fostering human relationships that acknowledge the other's point of view and place value on the multisided nature of human experience, democratic behavior in the classroom stays grounded in conversations to which we all feel comfortable contributing. In questioning the role of authority in the literature classroom and recognizing how listening might enrich our sense of the other, I find the lines of Peter's poem again resounding, "we are alive in each other." What might we all become as learners and teachers if we persisted in desiring democracy?

Chapter Two

Surviving in the
Hall of Mirrors

At the end of college, when I was contemplating beginning a life on the other side of the desk, America was in the midst of a teacher shortage. This helped me land a full-time teaching job without having had any practical teaching experience—just a straight liberal arts background, not one education course. In this first English job, I was to work with eleventh graders in a suburban Long Island high school, which was built to house more than 4,000 students. Reporting to the new teachers' orientation meeting on the Tuesday after Labor Day in 1965, I was given my class schedule, an empty lesson plan book, and a room key, and was told I would be teaching in 167A. Fine. Off I went down the long corridors to search for my room. As the numbers on the classroom doors got higher and higher—121, 133, 145—I found myself farther and farther from the center of the school. Where were these numbers leading me?

Finally, after several wrong turns, I arrived at my destination in splendid isolation. The administration had located me in the Girls' Auxiliary Gym—far from any regular classroom. Why was I being placed in quarantine? Did I already have that contagious disease called "noisy class"? Well, all right, let's get on with it, I thought to myself. After unlocking the door, I walked in and stared in amazement. Wherever I looked, all I could see was *myself.* In more prosperous and forward-looking times, the room had been designed to accommodate dance instruction. Full-length mirrors lined every wall.

What a disorienting environment, at least according to those more experienced than I. Time and again I was asked, "How can you stand it?" After the initial shock wore off, however, it became business as usual. Knowing no other surroundings for teaching, I soon felt quite at home. In fact, I began expecting to find mirrors in every classroom.

Not that the experience wasn't disconcerting at times. Meeting myself everyday, living with my reflection continually bouncing back at me—talk about feedback! From certain angles the classroom appeared awash with student faces. I could sense them to my right, to my left, even behind me, staring out from the walls. I couldn't hide from them or myself. Self-conscious, I frequently caught myself glancing at my appearance. Was my hair combed properly? My tie straight? My face animated? Was I gesturing too much or not enough?

Only later did all this self-absorption come to seem purposeful. The students and I, intently returning the gazes from those mirrors, admiring our reflection from every angle, were, in fact, creating and recreating ourselves. What impact were we having on others? In gesturing before those mirrors each day, we were trying to find out who we were. How might we recognize and acknowledge ourselves? And I very much empathized with these kids, because I had yet to establish myself as a teacher. On more than one occasion, minus my jacket and tie, I was stopped by some lady on the hall patrol and asked to identify myself. It reminded me of the time Gracie Allen went to the bank to cash a check and the teller asked her if she could identify herself. "I think so," Gracie replied and began fumbling around in her purse. Finally, she pulled out a make-up mirror, looked in it and said, "Yes, that's me."

Every day in school I saw students reflecting their performed accomplishments in the eyes of others as they jockeyed for peer acceptance and leadership. The judgments returned served an important mirroring function in shaping attitudes and behaviors, and in allowing students to seek their place in the scheme of the school. The images I and other teachers were sending out added to the students' repertoire of what it might mean to be an adult. These adult images, of course, were not always readily accepted, but, still, they hovered as a benchmark for the future. This may be one reason why students often feel compelled to return to their schools after graduation: to call attention to how and where they have moved and changed. What better way to do this than by contrasting themselves with teachers who have stayed put, continuing to teach the things that they teach. In returning to see the adults with whom they had worked in school, former students are using the adults as mirrors to sanction what has been altered in the new selves they have become and wish others to acknowledge.

My challenge was to make the English classroom serve some significant role in each student's desire to grow and change. In my hall of mirrors, however, something often went dead when we marched through the inherited procedures for reading literature. Whether it was book reports or thematic analyses or even open-ended discussions, there seemed little connection with what must have been foremost in their minds: their quest for identity and their attempt to develop some sense of personal power. What disturbed me about the undercurrent of student dissatisfaction I felt was that I believed myself to be on their side. I believed we were exploring the world together. Having taken on responsibility for improving their reading and writing, for encouraging their critical appreciation of literature, I didn't think I deserved their standoffish ways. Why was it so hard to connect my passion for reading literature with the students' pursuit of identity and esteem?

Often I felt extraneous to the natural course of their development—on the wrong side of an inevitable generation gap. With the endless interruptions and distractions of popular culture, let alone the public address system, they appeared to be little interested in me or the books I was supposed to get them to read. But perhaps it was my method that was interfering with their ability to join me in playing seriously with poems and stories. It took me a long time, even safely ensconced as I was in my haven of mirrors, to realize how this room, so full of reflections and responses, was curiously missing openness and community. What I had to understand was how I was contradicting my belief in democratic procedures by granting superior status to *my* responses and meanings when it came to the reading of literature. Yet, it was painful to give up this privilege. Indeed, I may never be able to do so completely.

At twenty-one years of age, in that particular hall of mirrors, I was unaware of having any special authority over the students. In fact, unprepared as I was, it didn't seem as though I was pursuing any restrictive agenda, except to keep a little order. Presumably, the conversation was free to move in ways beyond my control, and I felt no longing or compulsion to cover any particular works in the literary canon. Still, I didn't get it. I couldn't see the hidden structures that I was walking into and unconsciously reproducing. Simply allowing students the privilege of owning their own literary responses was not enough to capture their full interest, for they hungered, most of them, to be part of a constructive social enterprise. The actual workings of my classroom remained a mystery to me. I had no suspicion that unequal status relationships subtly determine the ways literary texts are handled in teaching situations, even when the parties are enlightened, experienced, and committed. All I had at my disposal were some warmed-over homilies about clarity, critical thinking, and the "unexamined life." This was not enough to put a democratic approach to reading literature into practice.

What did seem obvious, however, was that English majors tended to assume prior custodial rights to literature—to its joys and interpretations. Yet stories and their pleasures are for everyone. We share a common bond in needing to receive and interpret actively the endless swirl of cultural texts that surrounds us. Seemingly, many of my fellow English teachers had either forgotten or never perceived that literature should serve all citizens in a democracy. While other teachers were staring at a classroom full of students, I dwelt in a space full of mirrors and reflections. This made me question the usual predispositions of those English teachers who had grown accustomed to placing LITERATURE on a pedestal. In protest, I struggled to see literature as an ongoing initiation, an induction into a common conversation, a way of being with others, even those who have come from elsewhere and would rather be elsewhere. My hope was to entertain a vision of teaching English that combined coherence with uncertainty, thus validating the reading of literature as an ongoing social process and not as the transmission of someone else's knowledge.

Exploring the Sources of My Authority

How can I relax, when, as a teacher, my identity, my self-worth, depends on the way my authority is recognized by those I teach? Indeed, with literature as my subject, I keep finding myself in a paradoxical position with respect to authority: in the classroom, my principal claim to authority frequently consists in my having to give it up. This has nothing to do with discipline; rather, it has to do with giving students the freedom to discover who they are.

It is not difficult to affirm that the pleasures of reading literature go beyond merely recording the chronology of what happens in a story or a poem. The relating of indeterminate confusions of experienced emotions and motives, involving conflicting aesthetic and ethical concerns, is what really matters. Such things, of course, can never be reduced to multiple-choice questions. Once the answer is clear that no single answer will do or is "right," I can view the stories we are reading together in the classroom, both the students' stories and the ones in the books, from multiple perspectives. This allows me to see each story as an occasion for new possibilities, for disagreements about where the characters' motives and actions might lead us. But to do this I must relinquish my immediate authority over each text and openly share with students the inconsistencies, the contradictions, of response and interpretation. Still, it is difficult to be secure and flexible when contrary responses actually begin cropping up in the classroom.

In being too open or tentative with students, one basis of my authority—my knowledge of literature—is threatened. Indeed, some deep issue of ownership and control marks my undeniable anxiety. What I'm ostensibly being paid for as a professional are the facts that I know about stories and poems, and also the specific strategies for reading them. This is what I'm supposed to pass on to students. My identity, it sometimes seems, is tied up in being the "best" reader in class. Fortunately, what "best" means (the most knowledgeable? the most agile? the most open?) continues to elude me.

Who's in charge? What am I doing? These issues of authority seemed especially salient my first year of teaching. Barely older than my students, I was ambivalent about having just crossed the barrier between teacher and student. Indeed, on any given day my sympathies seemed located more on the students' side of the desk. Gradually, as I came to see the English class as a place for swapping and comparing stories of all sorts, I began to understand how tied up with authority was the question of my identity and the identities of my students. Openly exploring the works of literature before us, we were trying hard to determine who we were. Our disagreements reflected alternate stances toward experience and suggested the range of human relationships we were trying to sort out. Our comments about the stories we were reading and the stories we were telling became ways to embody and enact the beliefs and choices that constituted our identities.

But to take the position that personal responses to stories were central to what English teaching was all about risked getting me too close to the actual lives of my students. The more I encouraged them to come forward with their own responses, the less secure I became about assessing their achievements. I was bewildered when their responses not only didn't match mine, but seemed to come from a world totally foreign to me. On the other hand, it didn't take a genius to see that they were struggling with issues that really meant something to them. And the big problem that subsumed all the others came down to their relation to authority. We were still kids together. How were we going to receive the traditional patterns of social conduct being forced on us? What kind of adults might we become? On what basis were we going to establish our own autonomy and authority in the world?

The personal and social margins that students explored, when I had the courage to permit it in the classroom—which was still *mine,* not *ours*—were naturally filled with contradictions and ambiguities. In seeking friendship and fairness, for example, students were discovering that contrary feelings might reverse the best of intentions, that being outspoken wasn't always rewarded. Having opened up all this conflict for the purposes of literary inquiry, I saw that I had a special responsibility to support my students in their quest for maturity. Such a quest involved nothing less than learning to understand and live with the flaws of pervasive authority—defects and deceits, cruelty and greed—that literature was forever bringing to light, even as it was celebrating our potentially better selves. We needed to avoid becoming disillusioned when human frailty and weakness hindered efforts to create a more caring world. Accordingly, I believed the students might be better prepared to cope with the pretensions and hypocrisies of adult life if they began to uncover similar tendencies within themselves.

Should discovering the inconsistencies of authority, I wondered, be tantamount to rejecting it in whatever form? My authority was perhaps in doubt, but this didn't imply that anything goes. In the free-wheeling, confrontational 1960s, I felt we needed to learn together how to confront limitations and disappointments without yielding to despair or alienation, without turning skepticism into cynicism. Might we become more subtle in our perspectives and not simply dichotomize good and evil as a prelude to our own dogmatisms? Would frequenting the stories of literature, and writing their own, encourage these students to adopt a positive, ironic sensibility toward the ambiguities and uncertainties of existence? With these concerns in mind, one particular story, by Nathaniel Hawthorne, kept coming back to me. How might the crisis of human development faced by Young Goodman Brown help the students and myself in our own struggle to keep in balance the shortcomings and the virtues of human society?

Conversing with Young Goodman Brown

In the story of "Young Goodman Brown," first published in April 1835 in the *New-England Magazine,* Hawthorne invited his Puritan ancestors to speak across two centuries as a way of informing his own contemporary New England experience. Through Goodman Brown, Hawthorne archetypically dramatized that moment each of us faces while growing up—our loss of innocence. How will we react on discovering that our idealized image of the adult world diverges drastically from reality? This is not just a matter of losing our belief in Santa Claus or the Tooth Fairy. Rather, we find ourselves trying to cope with our emerging knowledge of danger in the world, danger from which parents can no longer protect us. And, unfortunately, too many children face this harsh reality without ever having experienced safety and security. In a land of freedom, where slavery once reigned, hunger and homelessness continue to exist side by side with wealth and luxury. And of every four persons who are homeless in our cities, one is a child. Abuse, injustice, inequity—for too many people this is the tangible substance of their lives. They never reach that point in the American dream where all citizens are free and equal to pursue their own ends for themselves. Given such conditions, is it possible for Goodman Brown's experience to speak across yet another century and reveal its relevance to us?

At the beginning of the story, Goodman Brown sets off on a mysterious journey into the darkness of the forest. Significantly, his wife, Faith, desires that he not go, lamenting, "A lone woman is troubled with such dreams and such thoughts that she's afeard of herself sometimes" (Hawthorne, p. 108). In her plea, and in the contrast of their given names, reside the thematic tension of the tale. *Goodman,* in focusing on good deeds, emphasizes the outer appearance of things. Remaining safely on the surface leads to literal mindedness. This consciousness means being out of touch with any knowledge of the body and its desires. Gradually, keeping his feelings hidden, Goodman enters a state of denial, rejecting—in Doubting Thomas fashion—all that cannot be seen. Contradictory emotions are to be avoided at all costs. Finally, Goodman turns to piety and righteousness.

Faith, in contrast, is concerned with a deeper awareness, an underlying sense of things that remains steadfast, despite the vicissitudes of immediate experience. Faith incorporates body into mind in order to accommodate *discrepancy* in the world. Faith holds securely beyond the surface appeals of fad and fancy. Accordingly, *goodness* without *faith* represents a frozen human sensibility. Alone, Goodman loses the ability to engage in good deeds, because for him the intentions behind them have become sullied, and, once doubt creeps in, virtue is dispatched forever. Faith, alone, fears her condition, for without deeds the confidence of her belief remains untested. Separated, good deeds wither and faith becomes blind.

"Young Goodman Brown" is about partnership, about keeping the mind in the body and the body in the mind. Only by resisting the temptation to fragment and dichotomize can we live a productive dialogue between goodness and faith.

So, here, I saw a major hurdle along the road toward maturity: I would have to negotiate a world of human motives and actions that inevitably fails to live up to my childhood expectations of perfection. Having discovered a secret consciousness of the body's claim on emotions, I needed to find ways of integrating this knowledge into public discourse and move beyond the surface of human encounters. Goodman, appearing confident and steadfast when I first meet him in the story, resolutely rejects that a person's opposing desires might need mediation. He strongly rebukes Faith for entertaining doubts about his journey (that classic solitary journey in search of meaning and value that is repeated so often in nineteenth-century American literature *written by men*—when all they had to do was stop and find solace in the connections of community). Faith can only reply, "Then God bless you! and may you find all well when you come back" (p. 108). But as I learn, Goodman is not blessed. By sunrise, when he returns again to the real world, he is a broken man. His rite of passage during the night of his dream quest has failed to lead him toward a mature and integrated response to experience.

Although I discover that Goodman Brown knew, all along, of the discrepancies between his deeds and his motives, what is at issue is how Goodman will confront the knowledge that such discrepancies exist for all persons. Each of us is born with the capacity to experience for ourselves. And, given the nature of our mental processes, we are destined to have more thoughts than we can ever possibly act out physically. Accordingly, there are always multiple intentions for any given act. This is merely another way of affirming that each and every event leads to any number of stories that might be told. The alignment of *idea* with *act* thus defies any single conclusion or generalization. Wonderfully equipped to think, rather than act, it is *not* natural for people to accept immediately the answers to the dilemmas of life that authority stands ready to supply. How often the "wise" advice of parents goes unheeded. The good acts that Goodman Brown viewed in his world appear innocent when motives are ignored. Trouble arises only when Goodman finds he cannot integrate the possibility of evil intentions. This is the dilemma of innocence, reconciling all those contradictory feelings that never quite align with the ideals that we wish to preserve.

Goodman Brown suspects he is journeying to sign a pact with the devil, but this knowledge is not something he can share openly with others, let alone his wife. "Methought as she spoke there was trouble in her face, as if a dream had warned her what work is to be done tonight. But no, no; 'twould kill her to think it. Well, she's a blessed angel on earth; and after this one night I'll cling to her skirts and follow her to heaven" (p. 109). Even as he wants to explore the darkness, Goodman, not his wife, is the one who can't bear unsavory thoughts, can't assert the mutuality of partnership. Since he cannot voice and share his doubts, his fears, Goodman ends by creating his own doom. Refusing to divulge the dark secret that he too has evil thoughts, Goodman can never find out that such secrets are common to all persons. Goodman has no monopoly on the terror of childhood secrets, secrets carried into adulthood.

In the midst of the forest, Goodman discovers that the minister, Deacon Gookin, and Goody Cloyse, who taught him his catechism, are all part of the devil's band, but he resolves to stand firm against their clutches, since he believes he can always fall back on his Faith. Alas, even she deserts him at the end of the journey, for it appears that, on the same night, his wife has also come to join this underworld fellowship. As the witches gathered, "it was strange to see that the good shrank not from the wicked, nor were the sinners abashed by the saints" (p. 118). All feelings of whatever sort must be given their due, if a person's experience is to remain whole. Finally, the dark figure presiding over this nefarious ceremony sums up the realities of the secret:

> Welcome, my children, to the communion of your race. Ye have found thus young your nature and your destiny. My children, look behind you! There are all whom ye have reverenced from youth. Ye deemed them holier than yourselves and shrank from your own sin, contrasting it with their lives of righteousness and prayerful aspirations heavenward. Yet here are they all in my worshipping assembly. This night it shall be granted you to know their secret deeds: how hoary-bearded elders of the church have whispered wanton words to the young maids of their households; how many a woman, eager for widows' weeds, has given her husband a drink at bedtime and let him sleep his last sleep in her bosom; how beardless youths have made haste to inherit their fathers' wealth; and how fair damsels—blush not, sweet ones—have dug little graves in the garden, and bidden me, the sole guest, to an infant's funeral. (p. 119)

Significantly, the assembled congregation is addressed as *children,* for the realm of adulthood that they are now about to enter is marked by a knowledge of good and evil. John Milton instructs us about what is unquestionably the central mythic story of Western culture: "It was called the tree of knowledge of good and evil from the event; for since Adam tasted it, we not only know evil, but we know good only by means of evil. For it is by evil that virtue is chiefly exercised, and shines with greater brightness" (Milton, p. 328). Significantly, this is a patriarchal version of the story. Women will not be denied knowledge of the conflicting sensations of the body, but men seemingly must be lured into tasting the fruit. A vision of caring and integration in this sense springs from a woman's refusal to accept divine authority, which in our particular religious mythology has ended up referring to God as the Father.

Since men have always tried to stand in as surrogates for this "original" authority, they have had to suppress women for attempting to raise an alternative and more natural story to the level of consciousness. Goodman's crisis in this instance grows out of his inability to see that the satisfactions of wholeness are only possible when dichotomies are transcended. He would keep purity isolated from the inevitability of death and decay, but in doing so he loses his final connection to purity itself. Good can only exist in relationship to evil. Without evil, without disruption in the world, good loses its very power to discriminate. But, even inside the boundaries of my own world, this paradox is never easily grasped. How often I struggle to make things appear all right on the surface and so deflect the pain and hurt of any number of primal disappointments.

Goodman's crisis of innocence turns into tragedy, because in the end he never compares stories with Faith. He travels alone outside the partnership of human conversation. The thoughts that burden him, while perhaps shameful, would have begun to dissipate in the presence of open communion with others, all of whom must necessarily deal with similar devils. The power of evil in this sense derives from exclusion. Only through disclosure might we hope to dispel its hold over us. Goodman, however, does not have enough faith to reveal the contents of his dreams, of his secret desires and ambitions. He cannot function in the human community with all its contradictions and transgressions. And after a long life thus, "they carved no hopeful verse upon his tombstone, for his dying hour was gloom" (p. 122). How instructive to my own devils is this tale. Trouble inevitably arises when I fail to test socially my *truth* about an encounter, a truth arrived at in splendid isolation. Yet it can be terrifying to live openly amid the contradictions raised by alternative perspectives.

In reading the story with others, the pivotal questions, naturally enough, seem to be ones of motivation and intent: Why doesn't young Goodman Brown tell his wife about what happened? Why doesn't he compare stories with her to see if what's in his mind really happened? If everyone seemed to be there at the witches' sabbath, why does he alone prefer to sulk and treat everyone with distrust? Comparing our responses to these issues keeps us focused on how we understand the perilous dichotomy between the individual and the community. The choice that this story emphasizes thus becomes one between isolation and negotiation. Goodman Brown could not remain open to others. Can we?

What Hawthorne has imagined in the experience of Goodman Brown serves to define, for me, what a life can be like when it fails to triumph over the loss of innocence and instead lives in fear that its own flaws will be found out by others. I take this to be a fable about the very real consequences of not rebounding from the discovery of the fallibility of authority. The shock of revelation demands all of one's courage to stay with the unravelling of truth and perfection.

Goodman Brown could not stay the course. He became all gloom because the idealistic position he took toward others could never be commensurate with what he recognized as his own shameful contents within. Belief for him was isolating. It did not provide a caring faith, because it was finally an all-or-nothing proposition. And while such a moral tale is, like education itself, partially wasted on the young, it can be a touchstone for the major crisis of growing up: How do I live with contradiction? How do I remain committed and cheerful in the face of ambiguity and exposed authority? How do I deal with the outbursts of immaturity that may strike at any age?

Chapter Three

Challenging Authority in the Classroom

When considering the issue of authority in the literature classroom, I find no compelling definition of what I'm supposed to be doing as a teacher. Although I'm responsible for helping students develop their abilities to read and write, the range of possible interpretations of literacy—and its attendant language skills—is so wide that almost any practice or prejudice can be justified. That is to say, there is no unifying set of principles to constrain what might happen in the English classroom.

Lacking a clear direction, teachers often lose touch with what compelled them to join our profession in the first place—a love of literature. Reading poems and stories of our own choosing constitutes for us a primary source of pleasure and understanding. When we take measure of how we are compelled by our own self-directed reading, we find ourselves beginning to act more effectively as teachers. We see, for instance, the importance of allowing students to play an active role in selecting what is read in the classroom, for this helps make the work we do together more meaningful for all of us.

While thinking about how literature might energize democratic encounters among teachers and students in the classroom, I discovered the following provocative definition offered by John Rouse: "English is the experience of myth and myth-making" (Rouse, p. 82). While I seem to be unsuccessful in convincing others of its merits, such a definition helps me stay centered on the democratic satisfactions possible in the teaching of literature.

The definition begins with the word *experience*—not a readily circumscribed concept because of its common, everyday usage. Experience signifies a conscious transaction between a person and his or her surroundings, a transaction involving both time present and time past. Initially, there is a sense of immediate and active indwelling. What is happening to us exists in the present moment. At any given moment, however, our sensibility also draws on the accumulated lessons of our personal history. Our experience of current actions and events thus always reflects something inherited from our past.

From the perspective of the psychologist George Kelly, experience results from a person's primary intellectual activity, creating or constructing a *representation* or meaning where previously there had been only nameless events passing by willy-nilly. In other words, people pay little attention to the events surrounding them until these events have been marked off or identified in some way and so become deliberately built into what we call a person's *experience.* Buying a red Saturn suddenly makes us aware of all the other red Saturns on the road. Or think of new parents discovering to their dismay that their home, which previously was perfectly suitable for two adults, now is in need of child-proofing.

The constructive quality of experience means it is not something that can be done for us by another person. In other words, individuals must be involved in the making of the categories that determine their experience; they can't just be handed them. So, already, Rouse's definition of English, with its emphasis on *experience,* would rule out any kind of transmission teaching that does not recognize the learner's need to be an active participant in the classroom.

Myth too presents us with complications. Myth is the source of all literature. It springs from the core of our imaginative capacity to explain the world around us. Thus we need to define myth in a way that emphasizes how it functions as a basic mental process through the medium of personal and cultural stories. At its deepest levels, a myth or story mediates some discontinuity that lies at the heart of our cultural values. The discontinuities that give rise to myths—birth/death, generosity/greed, female/male, peace/war, listening/speaking, student/teacher—help create the moral and ethical space in which humans struggle to maintain and revise their beliefs. Myths can prompt a dialogue between those opposites that define the paradoxes or tensions of human existence. In doing so they can serve as a tool for self-discovery. "Young Goodman Brown," for example, not only plays with the struggle between good and evil, it also expresses additional tensions in our perspectives, such as those between inside/outside, depth/surface, concrete/abstract, body/mind, feelings/head.

People don't just do things; we have moral and ethical reasons for doing them. However, these reasons or motives are complicated by the opposing sides competing for our loyalty. Thus, to *experience myth* or, substituting the key words, to *read literature,* is not just a casual venture, but one that provokes a reader into contemplating the reasons behind events. Every position enacted or evoked would like to silence its defining opposite. In a man's world, for instance, it remains difficult to be heard as a woman. Even a field such as medical research privileges the male body, with its particular anatomy and ailments, as the standard. Staying with the complexities of the tensions between contrasting opposites is difficult, but to do so represents our acknowledgment of the contrary voices that democracy fosters.

Once *myth* is understood in terms of the crisscross of values and intentions, *myth making* can be seen as its complement. It is students creating, sharing, and criticizing their own mythic tensions, whether they appear in narrative or expository form. Through their participation in the natural cycles of production and reception, students celebrate and extend their own constructive and reflective capacities, and in doing so they come to make sense of their world in a way that allows room for comprehending the other. Comprehension, in this sense, values the collaborative social dimension of reading and writing.

What interests me about this definition of English is the underlying set of democratic teacher-learner relationships it serves to uncover when I actually try to carry out its precepts. For some time now (beginning perhaps in the 1960s, if not earlier), persons teaching literature—from an elementary language arts teacher to a university English professor—have, as I have been suggesting, found themselves in an untenable position. Their authority in relation to the language, to the text, and to the student has been in decline. They have become trapped between the dogmatism of a frightened and judgmental public and the contingent relativity of the academy. Of course, many people, including parents, employers, and senior faculty members, maintain a clear vision that the role of the English teacher is solely to transmit the etiquette of standard dialects and correct textual interpretations. On the other hand, scholars in the fields of language and literary studies point to a contrasting reality: *All* dialects are properly labelled as non-standard, rather than substandard and *all* readings might be viewed as existing in productive

conversation with each other. Although conversations that democratically open the text to all readers provide an opportunity for
some teachers to expose privilege and injustice, the traditional curriculum quickly interposes standards of routine and neutrality. The
regimen of skill and drill and a return to the "basics" lead the
charge. Disembodied and decontextualized words and sentences
mark an English class that ignores both the confirming and dislocating "experience of myth and myth-making."

This is not just a matter of exchanging rhetorical skirmishes in
the current version of the culture wars; there are real consequences
for students/readers. On the one side are those teachers who believe
they can keep value considerations out of the classroom by asserting their control over what a poem or story means—they can function as stand-ins for the absent author. On the other side are those
teachers who not only feel secure enough to allow value disputes to
come into the classroom, but who believe the meanings of texts are
continually being socially constructed. In the first instance, acts of
interpretation must fully square with an author's presumed (or ap-
parent) intentions. In the second, the tale is to be trusted, not the
teller, which implies that no one really has the final word when it
comes to reading. Meanings, it is assumed, arise from a reader's
transaction with a poem; they are not imposed from without.

Encouraging Open Acts of Reading

Seeing English as "the experience of myth and myth-making" helps
me to focus on the tension between similarity and difference that
marks a student's engagement with a literary text. Perhaps the reader
begins with an unsettled feeling, but in some way the end result
should be *confidence*. Reading may disturb students so that they consider changing their positions or stances in the world. This, of
course, can be severe when social class boundaries or traditional gender scripts are being transgressed. But even when this is not the case,
the adage "You can't go home again" contains an important truth.

For development and change to occur, I must see the text as
more than information, reading as more than decoding. Then I can
frame the text as an irritant, a grain of sand in the oyster's home.
Working dialectically, the text confronts a reader with both similarity and difference. By avoiding any focus on decontextualized
skills, I try to stay with the more profound dislocations provoked in
students by their literary transactions. To do this, I need to remain
open to the complex and often contradictory relationships with au-

thority that must be worked through as each student searches for and constructs an identity.

My challenge is to uncover the argument of individual student myths and to analyze their claims and conclusions in relation to the immediate supporting evidence and to evidence that may have been suppressed. In this regard, it is useful to acknowledge how arguments and evidence rely on people sharing similar sets of conventions and convictions. The social values embodied in myths are most powerful when they remain invisible to us. A myth (story) appears convincing because it establishes some "logical" relationship between its evidence and its assertion. In many cases the author will fool us into thinking that this relationship, which is actually *psychological,* describes a real cause-and-effect connection in the world. Accordingly, a tension exists between the logical and the psychological, and this tension confuses students not initiated into the official scripts of the academy. For example, the teacher comment "Logical relationship?" written in the margin of a student composition seldom refers to any violation of the rules of formal logic. Instead, it seeks to enforce the injunction that the student had better reproduce the "correct" world view. Given the dominating power of my position as teacher, if I don't want students merely to feign agreement with my perspective, I must work hard at recovering the spaces between us in which lie the tacit stories that mark our differing world constructions. Until the tacit, and perhaps competing, myths of both student and teacher are brought out into the open and given expression, democratic pluralism remains impossible.

As much as even the most brilliant, learned teacher prepares in advance, in the presence of an open text and a new set of students, some novel interpretation is bound to emerge. Lessons come alive when a teacher learns to incorporate the interpretive agility of the other readers in the class. Yet to reach a level of confidence where we're able to let the text provoke student reading and response, we need to recognize the choices facing us. First, we can suppress student novelty (resistance) and any suggestion of play, and thus maintain the authority of our preordained interpretations, claiming, finally, that this is the information that we as teachers have been charged with transmitting. Second, we can appear to welcome novelty and pass the full authority for interpretation over to the students, a form of throwing up our hands and trying to exit gracefully from the center of authority. Or, third, we can cultivate novelty, insisting that this very act of transcending our current position of power as teacher is what constitutes our true teaching authority. Our task thus becomes redefined as one of fostering the authority of others, instead of displaying and enforcing our own. Choosing this last position also allows us to build interpretations in common with the students, which in turn helps us to come to terms with the anxiety we often feel when confronting the relativity of meaning.

All three teacher stances will exist as long as the reader-author (reader-teacher) relationship in the realm of teaching literature remains unsettled. Although the drift toward democratic openness may be inevitable—with youth feeling free to supplant age by virtue of its new interpretive independence—wise elders seldom willingly relinquish the power that derives from their wisdom. They resist turning over control of the poem, which, of course, is unable to speak for itself. Still, once authority is seen as residing in the book-reader relationship, and not solely in the person of the "wise" teacher, this dominant hierarchical structure of the transmission of interpretations, which has governed education for so long, becomes increasingly outmoded. Yet, instead of replacing one tyranny with another, open acts of reading, which involve readers staying with texts no matter where they might lead, help induce teachers and students to work in concert with each other.

The Dilemma of Dominating Readings

All too often students who risk novelty in interpretation, even at advanced levels, will be quickly put in their place. One such disturbing incident, which a student told me recently, suggests how the authority issue is further compounded with matters of gender. Are women, even more than men, being forced into interpretive straitjackets? In a class assigned to interpret a seventeenth century poem that featured the word *dying*, this female student decided not to restrict her interpretation to the safe boundaries of the death theme, but chose instead to strike out into the area of loving, even going so far as to mention the unity of "the sperm and the egg," and the problem of male impotency. During a conference with the student, after the paper was returned, the professor, clearly nervous about the subject matter that had been elicited, acknowledged to the student how well the paper was written, but said he had lowered the grade to a B+ because her interpretation, which was only the *secondary* one, had supplanted what should have been the primary understanding of the poem. Needless to say, this left the student in a quandary regarding her own originality and how to play it safe by regurgitating orthodoxy.

As a result of ever-increasing scholarly study and competition, it is not surprising to find the common reader easily overwhelmed by the pyrotechnics of "professional" readers. Thus, despite the lip service paid to reader-response criticism and reception theory, reading strategies have emerged that reestablish the preeminence of the reading experience and "wisdom" of the professor. These strategies take at least two forms. First, I can talk in some restricted code, so that no one outside my narrow, interpretive community can understand me. David Lodge sums up the calamity of this academic maneuver:

> The tragic irony [is] that English and literary studies have reached a point in their theoretical development when they've become incapable of communicating to the layman at the very historical moment when they've most needed to justify their existence. The brightest and most innovative people in literary criticism are as impenetrable as nuclear physicists. The left-wing intelligentsia is trapped in a kind of ghetto that only they understand, and so can't bring any leverage to bear on the body politic.[1]

And yet the stock of high theory soars in the groves of academe, especially as it seems to subvert more and more the immediate pleasures of reading. Second, after acknowledging the importance of a student reader's role in bringing *contextual* information to the act of interpretation, I can then endlessly demonstrate how much better I am in supplying such information. Under these circumstances, how can any reader—let alone a student reader—avoid lacking confidence when inundated by the encyclopedic references that literary critics are able to call up even when reading the most obscure text? For example, Harold Bloom's own gargantuan readings of intertextuality (see Bloom, 1973), however brilliant and suggestive, risk intimidating beginning readers with a terminal attack of the kind of anxiety of influence that he is revealing in his writings about other writers.

It seems that the desire of earlier critics, such as E. D. Hirsch (see Hirsch, 1967), to establish the original intent of the author is now being replaced with something that is much more difficult to resist. This new way of keeping authors from communicating directly with an audience of readers involves a teacher insisting that interpretation be suspended until all the "necessary" cultural and historical referents are in place. To attain this more "satisfying" reading, one is supposed to recover the original conditions out of which the text was written, including, ultimately, how the text may be connected to any number of other texts and how the reader's position toward the text is socially determined. As important as such scholarship may be in both challenging and enriching one's readings, it presents the danger of inserting yet another layer of knowledge that must be mastered before the reader can ever get to having a response. For how can any student be expected to marshal the referential resources that expert readers have at their command, even in the case of deceptively straightforward texts? Instead of working toward increasingly responsible readings of the text, it is more likely that many readers, by now exasperated, will long since have abandoned their pleasure.

This pattern of teacher dominance is dramatically underscored by one of my graduate students in her reflections on the powerful ways in which her teachers interfered with and controlled her own reading authority:

> I have found myself in many of my high school and college classes, sitting back and letting the teacher define the work according to their own intellectual standards. I then would take this knowledge of what the teachers expected the students to get out of the work and reorganize my own insights of the work in a pattern corresponding with the teacher's words. I did not realize this at the time, but looking back on my early educational experiences I see how much the teachers' lecturing on "background information" limited my understanding of the text according to my own experiences. (personal communication)

She illustrates this process by recounting an episode in her sophomore year of college when a teacher assigned Toni Morrison's *Sula*.

> My professor wanted our understanding of the text to be on a college level as he stated, so prior to the reading of the novel he taught us a two week segment about the deconstructionist Derrida. He went into his own interpretation of the novel based on Derrida's theory of the decentering of the universe. When it came time to read the novel I found it hard to appreciate Morrison's style of writing. I could not even concentrate on analyzing the character Sula according to my own beliefs about her reasons for acting in the manner she did. Instead I wanted to please the teacher and knew that in order to do so I must interpret Sula's character according to Derrida's deconstructionist theory.

Fortunately, this student was able to regain her composure as a reader; after graduating from college, she read the novel on her own. This time, as she says, "With no pressure from any teacher to analyze the work according to their interpretation, I was able to use my own experiences to enjoy the novel." This positive ending, however, comes from an individual who is interested in reading and wants to pursue a career teaching literature. What of all those students who choose never to read serious fiction again, having been adversely influenced by the intrusions of an overpowering teacher?

When I raise doubts about the potential tyranny of contextualized readings, I am not implying that one should be painted into a corner of ignorance. It is nonsensical to deny the role played by context (codes) in shaping the interpretations possible from a reading. Indeed, contrary to those who talk about the radical indeterminacy of meaning or who, like Norman Holland, consider that each reader is finally isolated in their own idiosyncratic patterns of response, I take it that we are all referring to the same marks on the page. Our very membership in the culture depends on us reading socially in this way. Unfortunately, however, contextual approaches dominated by the teacher's display of knowledge can quickly yield a scale of reading adequacy, one that privileges those student readers who have gathered the most information about the text. The rest are forced to drown in a sea of authoritatively positioned voices.

This I see as a central struggle of our profession: How do we maintain a productive balance between our expertise and knowledge as teachers/readers and the evoked experience of the poem that students/readers need to have for themselves? Before our interference occurs, students need to explore their own mythic relationship to the text, navigating the words on their own or with groups of trusted peers. Only then perhaps will they feel safe enough to begin an excursion into the otherwise daunting world of scholarship and criticism. In short, demolish all the barriers that keep students from getting involved with the text. When art sits on a pedestal, viewers or readers genuflect rather than become engaged as equals. Student readers need to discover that their interpretive enthusiasm lies within, just as Jerry Reilly found out when crowds began flocking to his Museum of Bad Art in Roxbury, Massachusetts: "Because it's the Museum of Bad Art, people aren't afraid to give their opinion. In fact, they talk passionately about the art. You never see that in a regular museum."[2]

Not forced to obey and submit, students may enter a dialogue with what professional readers have to say about the poem under consideration, a dialogue that can expand and refine their initial understanding of the words on the page. Once a text has been entertained at the intimate level of a primary reading[3]—with all of its confusions, false steps, and personal associations—an interest may be sparked that leads to a wider consideration of what the critics and scholars think. A vertical relationship to authority, in this instance, is replaced by a horizontal one, because the critics/scholars are no longer positioned to lock out the student-reader's response. Entering the wider conversation obliquely in this way, student readers are more open to having the satisfactions of their own readings challenged, confirmed, and extended.

No rule or formula will ever establish exactly when we should intercede with background knowledge that will help inexperienced readers grasp more fully both the immediate meanings signaled by the text and the larger cultural messages located within it. Recently, I was having students read a poem by Peter Davison, "I Hardly Dream of Anyone Who Is Still Alive," when it became clear that they had no idea who was being named by the poet. Red Auerbach, for instance, drew a blank, and when John Berryman appeared, one student confused him with John Barrymore, the actor, and started seeing images of dramatic productions in the poem. Once again, I saw I could take nothing for granted. Initially, wanting them to come up with their own readings free of my interference, I remained silent. It was difficult, however, not to blurt out information about Red Auerbach chomping on his cigar during those many championship years when he coached the Boston Celtics basketball team or not to mention the suicide of the poet John Berryman. Eventually, I did speak up, and then as a group we talked about the consequences of being completely oblivious to the poet's reference system. The problem, as they saw it, was one of learning to ask questions during the process of reading and not depend on predigested context notes. Still, the timing and need for information can change from situation to situation once student readers learn that their primary responses are an integral part of the reading equation in the classroom.

As a teacher I can encourage students to stay with what the poem or story says to them, not chase after the conclusions of others and end up in dependent confusion. Lingering awhile with their primary readings, students develop an independence and confidence that they can draw on when they join the wider reading conversation. Yet, despite my teaching maneuvers aimed at inviting more readers into the conversation, especially in an age that has supposedly discovered the reader, grave threats to the authority vested in me as the teacher remain. These threats spring to life whenever students enter the drama of the classroom spouting alternative myths regarding human behavior and experience, exposing generational and cultural gaps where knowledge of Red Auerbach disappears on the other side. Such reversals of logic can be especially unsettling when I have already committed so deeply to a given myth or theory that I have become emotionally attached to it. To scrutinize my own ideas about the world may expose inconsistencies in a core belief, one that previously allowed me to make sense of things. Caught off guard, do I really want to be forced to reconsider my line of thinking, which I then might have to admit has frozen into dogma? And, even if openness is possible, isn't such a reconsideration of my beliefs both risky and disconcerting since the end result might be change? Do I want to become a student all over again?

Notes

1. Quoted 16 October 1989. "The Tools a Writer Used for Building An Industrial Novel,"*New York Times,* section C, p. 15.

2. Reported by Frauenfelder, Mark. July 1995. "Canvas Catastrophes." *Wired* 3(7): 50.

3. For a discussion of the distinction between primary and secondary acts of reading, see Pradl, 1994. Pp. 233–44.

Chapter Four

Students Speaking Up
for Themselves

When the text becomes open in my classes, students challenge my authority in four ways. They contest my knowledge, resist my agenda, question my procedures, and overthrow my paradigms. In each instance, my best defense is simply to constrain students from speaking up. Beyond enforcing silence in this direct manner, I also have the option of signaling to the students that I am not taking what they have to say seriously. Barring these strategies, however, with an open text students gradually realize that they must share responsibility for learning, that multiple perspectives mark our democratic enterprise, and so they come to assert their own agency.

Contesting My Knowledge

Calmly, urgently, or sarcastically, students demand, "Have you read . . . ?" or "Did you know that?" or "That's not right." Time for the bluff or a bit of deftly maneuvered back-pedaling. Rare are the moments when I can directly say, "No, I don't know that," and, better yet, add, "Tell me about it." This forces me to acknowledge that it's never just information that's being learned, but some *stance* toward that information. This contention about knowledge does not exclusively characterize older students. Young children, when we listen to them properly, surprise us with all kinds of insights and reversals. They give us clues as to what they're thinking and feeling, which we might not surmise if we fail to provide a forum for their words.

When students keep contradicting our messages or ask too many questions, they certainly try our patience. Nancy Sommers describes one such college freshman who "didn't like the time of the class, didn't like the reading list, didn't seem to like me." It seemed that nothing would make him content with the flow of the class:

> "If this is a class on the essay," he asked the first day, "why aren't we reading real essayists like Addison, Steele, and Lamb?" On the second day, after being asked to read Annie Dillard's "Living Like Weasels," David complained that a weasel wasn't a fit subject for an essay. "Writers need big subjects. Look at Melville. He needed a whale for *Moby Dick*. A weasel—that's nothing but a rodent." And so it continued for a few weeks. (Sommers, p. 425)

Struggling to maintain her equanimity in class, Sommers secretly wished this unending source of irritation would just go away. But then she made an important discovery, sensing in this irritating student "a kindred spirit, someone else who needed to question authority" (p. 425). Ironically, provocative students actually end up supporting positions that we on other occasions might have claimed as our own. It seems our injunction to change the world—"Don't accept things the way they are"— doesn't always extend to what's being said and done in our own classrooms. How much better to say directly to students, "Thank you for reminding me!"

Resisting My Agenda

My ignorance is not my only vulnerable point. In the midst of a class discussion—one that is operating within the safe boundaries of a pre-established topic and a set of conversational conventions—questions might be genuinely open ended and students may be invited to challenge the argument as it's been presented so far. Here I'm openly encouraging students to detect logical inconsistencies. Under such classroom circumstances I deliberately provoke students to learn by disagreeing with me and other students—a devil's advocate notion of the teacher's role. Yet this script too is highly constrained, spelling out an unwritten code of conduct: Students are *not* allowed to raise objections about the topic or the form of discussion.

One day, in a language course, a rather hostile student (from my perspective at least) stood up in the middle of class and tried to instigate a revolt. He felt the particular exercise we were discussing—looking at sentence structures and derivations—contradicted earlier messages I had given the students, messages he felt had invited him to inquire openly about language, not learn grammatical rules by rote in order to complete a teacher assignment. In very direct terms, he urged the other students to join him in walking out, and then he left in a fury. It was a moment beyond words. I could feel the discomfort in the other students who, while not wishing to challenge my authority, had nonetheless just heard voiced some of their own misgivings about the drift of the lesson.

As upset and disturbed as I was, I needed to find a way to reintegrate this student into the class, even though he had supposedly severed all the rules of student-teacher decorum. In other words, how could I reconstrue the situation as one of learning, not of face saving? How might we share equally in the responsibility for reinventing our learning conversation? Fortunately, before the next class. the student and I were able to talk out our conflicting intentions. Thus, when he returned to the group, we again openly discussed the assignment with all the students and made some adjustments in the light of other complaints being voiced. While this example may seem extreme, when openness is invited, the teacher must be flexible and accepting when it comes. Indeed, many times I have felt a sinking feeling of frustration during class when students attack my various sacred cows about democracy and the teaching of literature, and I have not always refrained from adopting an adversarial stance.

Questioning My Procedures

Because in one sense all the routines of a classroom are arbitrary, regardless of how they are justified, the idea that everyone is entitled to their own opinion can easily degenerate into quarrels about the readings, the written assignments, the due dates and attendance regulations, and, of course, the grades—"That's not how we're doing it in my other classes!" For example, while the whole issue of grades can be sidestepped (perhaps give everyone an A), the intersubjective quality of open literature classes inevitably reveals the shaky ground on which a teacher arrives at final assessments. Like most teachers, I've encountered any number of grade complaints, yet handling one case never quite prepares me for the next. Again I find myself caught between encouraging learning relationships with students and then being institutionally responsible for judging their competence. I may not be "smarter," may not even "know" more than my students—and both the students and I may openly ac-

knowledge this—but my institutional position as judge and evalua-
tor can serve to stifle uninhibited conversation that might otherwise
exist if we were all peers in the classroom.

Here is Marion, one of my graduate students, writing about the
ambivalent feelings that arise when new classroom arrangements
clash with old student habits of dependency:

> I have really enjoyed the freedom; however, now that the end of
> the semester is approaching, I find myself anxious in a new, un-
> usual way. In classrooms where authority is handled in a tradi-
> tional way, I am usually pretty sure of where I stand by this time
> in the semester. In this class, because I have been given the oppor-
> tunity (and burden) to design my own requirements, I am not sure
> how I'm doing. Have I done enough work? How am I going to be
> graded? In a class where I'm told what to do, I am very good at
> doing it. This class is different, because I am not entirely sure what
> the criteria are—I set up some of my own, but how does the
> teacher really feel about those criteria, and does he see me as ful-
> filling them? (personal communication)

What I learn about my own authority from such students is not always pleasant. Clearly, in extending freedom, I've not always been
adequately sensitive to the contradictory feelings that such freedom arouses in students. As this student expressed it, some of the
new responsibilities led to worries that took away from the time
she might otherwise have spent learning, and so the experience
was, in Marion's words, "both empowering and upsetting." This, of
course, remains part of my intention, to raise irritations and misgivings, and so encourage students to take charge of their own
learning. But, often, I don't clarify enough what's going on; I don't
allow for reflective responses to the process of change as it is occurring. In this instance, I didn't attend enough to the part of this student that was feeling a desire for, as she expressed it, "some hard,
set rules to follow." How different if we had corresponded earlier
and I had responded:

> Playing with the frames of authority is scary for me too. I think
> there are times when I freeze up after having loosened the reins. I
> know I have subtle ways of cracking an invisible whip to show
> that even as I let you be free, it's *me* who's really in charge, if not
> in control. In writing to me, you help me see that together we need
> to consider more explicitly what it feels like to take responsibility
> for setting your own agenda. For I don't want you to be isolated in
> this—you're not alone. I hope we can find ways of working to-
> gether on setting problems and ways of assessing how everyone's
> progressing. Sharing your fears shows me how much more I have
> to listen and in turn share some of my own apprehensions.

How far to go in opening up the classroom remains a delicate issue when questioning authority is legitimized. Education, of course, is not inevitably an occasion for rebellion, but certainly many works of literature directly challenge established authority, and this is an irony I try not to lose sight of in my own teaching.

Overthrowing My Paradigms

In an open literature classroom the entire world view of the teaching-learning situation, including its content and how it is being conducted, is called into question. While this may only be a more severe version of the *agenda* challenge, the following story, related by one of my graduate students, illustrates, I think, the quantum leap that is involved when the cross-generational aspect of textual interpretation is highlighted. This student, a history major, found himself confronting a professor whose ideas and values at every turn were contrary to his own. For him, the professor's view of history was completely "reactionary, outdated and tiresome." Although the course was supposed to be a colloquium, the professor lectured endlessly. Seemingly fearful of what might come up in discussion, he frequently went off on tangents and related reminiscences and anecdotes. During the last class of the semester, grouped with seven others around a large, coffin-shaped table, this student found himself on the edge:

> I went head-to-head with him in a historical argument and won clearly. I had the chance to go for the kill and leave him looking like a complete fool before the class, but I didn't. It wasn't pity, it was the look of sheer panic and fright in his face as he tried to cover himself, that stopped me. It was an unreal situation, but it really did happen, and I would have to say it was one of the most thrilling moments in my life as a graduate student. (personal communication)

Was this only egotistical males in mortal combat? Or did the student have a right to overthrow this professor who was in the business of history because of nostalgia and an old-fashioned attachment to the great figure stories of the past? This moment of conflicting styles and paradigms certainly scares me into taking a second look at what is going on around me in class. There have been times when I thought I was setting up an active learning situation only to discover that students were construing it as an occasion for me to be on display. When captive students believe the lesson is merely an excuse for me to establish a platform for spouting my views, then it is time to share what each of us thinks about the possible roles of authority in *our* classroom.

Authority: A Middle-Class Anxiety?

Finally, to what extent are authority issues merely class-bound phenomena? According to Barbara Ehrenreich's analysis, the authority that has come to reside in the academy serves the vested interest that middle-class people have in *professionalism,* an institutional concept and state of mind they have invented:

> In every field, professionalization was presented as a reform, a bold new measure aimed at replacing guesswork and tradition with science and rationality. But it was also an economic strategy. . . . Through professionalization, the middle class sought to carve out an occupational niche that would be closed both to the poor and to those who were merely rich. (Ehrenreich, p. 78)

The particular brand of authority relations dictated by education in formal school settings depends not on groups, but on individuals; so it is not surprising that everything from discipline to achievement boils down to single student units. Thus, the classroom becomes a crucial proving ground for the middle class to work through its lover's quarrel with authority. As Ehrenreich suggests, "the middle class still fancies itself a set of self-determining individuals, not a group driven by common interests and instincts" (p. 238).

But to expose the authority of individual teachers over individual students through the dynamics of textual interpretation is to risk bringing down the whole house of cards. When "the wisdom of professors" is challenged, and along with it "the moral legitimacy of the university," then, as Ehrenreich suggests, the hegemony of professionals appears at risk. Not respecting their claim to authority is tantamount to questioning the whole status of the middle class. Indeed, "physicians and attorneys, sociologists and scientists would have no more standing in the world than mechanics or secretaries" (p. 77). Referring to the turmoil experienced on many campuses during the late 1960s, Ehrenreich concludes,

> When students challenged the authority of their professors, when they questioned the validity and relevance of the knowledge from which that authority was said to be derived, they struck at the fundamental assumptions of their class. Judged in the context of that class and its interests, they were guilty of nothing less than treason.

> They had exposed, in however inarticulate a fashion, the conceit on which middle-class privilege rests: We know more, and are therefore entitled to positions of privilege and authority. (p. 81)

If Ehrenreich's analysis even approximates the social myth under which many literature teachers work, it is no wonder that we experience great difficulty with patterns of behavior that grow out of collaboration.

In the classroom, my nervousness about democratic collaboration relates to my inability to tolerate ambiguity when it comes to textual interpretation. I'd prefer not having to face—without an established, predefined hierarchy of power and authority —the task of sorting out exactly where I fit as a teacher within the overlapping circles of knowledge, competence, and responsibility that define my profession. I'd like to avoid the problem of relativism in a postmodern, pluralistic world. It's a threat and a burden to derive my authority from horizontal networking, especially when previously I've seen my role as supporting vertical lines of control. For teachers caught in the drive for middle-class professionalism, how real are these anxieties? How difficult will it be to change their classroom stances? Can we meet the democratic challenge and find ways to assuage the very real discomforts we feel as we go about learning to construe openness as an opportunity, not a threat?

Chapter Five

Rethinking Our Privilege and Status

The kinds of authority that involve power and control require hierarchical or vertical arrangements among people. This authority to regulate the behavior of others depends principally on methods of *exclusion.* From our own self-centered perspective as supposedly equal citizens in a democracy, we seldom dwell much on this problem, because it seems that the particular power we derive from exclusion is mostly obtainable by everyone. There seems to be an endless supply of persons or groups that can be pushed aside for our benefit. But once the structure of exclusion is uncovered, it becomes clear how often we ourselves are forced to the outside.

People in a liberal democracy often try to justify exclusion by pointing to some personal limitation in the individual. Thus, exclusion is not supposed to be based on group membership whether by race, gender, class, age, disability, or even sexual orientation (wealth may be a different matter, of course). Instead, it's just some idiosyncratic difference or, better yet, some kind of difference of talent or competence, especially of an academic variety. In the end, we partition the world in an infinite number of ways—from honor students and football teams to nursing homes and private clubs—hoping to gain some advantage in finding areas where we belong, but others don't. In doing so we think to ourselves, I can exclude you, but you can't exclude me.

Democracy disrupts the finality of such partitions. Customs and beliefs that divide are gradually supposed to become anomalous as society continues to evolve. Democracy encourages a regular examination of the inequities involved in arrangements of exclusion. However justified a particular grouping may appear to its beneficiaries, those concerned with democratic relationships keep raising issues of fairness and parity, as they try to look beyond the indulgences of selfish profits and short-term gains. This is opposed to a fixed conservative position that nostalgically clings to the privileges of the past, viewing any changes that involve more inclusion as additional evidence of the continuing decline of authority. Persons with such sentiments fiercely resist letting more people onto the playing field.

Arguments for freedom of association, and the fact that distinctions make for a rich variety of opportunities in our culture, should not be used to confuse the exclusion issue. Individual groupings of citizens are supposed to occur on the basis of positive avocation rather than negative personal prejudice. As John Burnheim contends, "In such a community rights to exclude others would be less valued than rights to be included in those groups one wanted to join" (Burnheim, p. 182). But it's not so easy to support such open access once we've grown up and come to reify the differences we see around us. Generally it's too late to overturn a prejudice slowly ingrained over the years. Thus, we must expose the habits of exclusion early on. In schools, we need to live by a code of conduct that explicitly confronts the private tendency of students to fence others out. We must affirm that, in this public space, we proceed by inclusion, not by exclusion.

You Can't Say, "You Can't Play"

The simple wisdom and courage of such a radical position is dramatized in yet another of those remarkably unpretentious books by Vivian Gussin Paley. In *You Can't Say You Can't Play*, Paley tells the story of how she went about trying to change the rules of interpersonal groupings in her kindergarten class. Struck one day with the deep unfairness of the pattern of social relations that allowed one child to reject another child's request to play, she decides to work carefully at shifting the understandings and scripts that make such exclusionary behavior acceptable. Having reached a decision, Paley moves firmly and deliberately, yet she is also careful not to be authoritarian. Thus she does not set down her new rule, You can't say you can't play, dictatorially with no discussion or dissent allowed. Instead, she gradually generates support by educating the children in her care to understand the benefits of this rule and to explore ways to enact it. In a questioning and invitational manner, she slowly builds consensus. As she tells one girl, "This wouldn't be the sort of rule you'd get punished for breaking. If you don't follow what the rule requires, then . . . well, you just think about it and talk about it some more. It isn't a matter of punishing someone, it's more a case of protecting someone" (Paley, p. 113). Sensitive to the conflicting feelings surrounding issues of exclusion, Paley also invents a serial story about the adventures of a magpie in a magical kingdom. During the course of the year, she tells her children this myth as a means of reparation for the particular concerns they are feeling.

Paley expresses her democratic social agenda explicitly. She's concerned with fairness, but the core of her faith goes back to feelings and relationships:

> Certain children will have the right to limit the social experiences of their classmates. Henceforth a ruling class will notify others of their acceptability, and the outsiders learn to anticipate the sting of rejection. Long after hitting and name-calling have been outlawed by the teachers, a more damaging phenomenon is allowed to take root, spreading like a weed from grade to grade. (p. 3)

Children, she knows from long experience, "yearn for explanations of sadness," and therefore they welcome an open consideration of how people are being treated in school, even though, initially, only four of twenty-five children—the rejected ones—find the new rule appealing:

> Being told you can't play is a serious matter. It hurts more than anything else that happens in school, and distractions no longer work very well. Everyone knows the sounds of rejection: You can't play; don't sit by me; stop following us; I don't want you for a partner; go away. These would be unforgivable insults if spoken at a faculty meeting, but our responses are uncertain in the classroom. (pp. 14–15)

Arguing that the classroom belongs to every child—and therefore is not a private space, like home—Paley sees what happens in free play as violating the democratic ideal of equal participation in our public places. "In truth, free acceptance in play, partnerships, and teams is what matters most to any child" (p. 21). Thus she sees a fundamental value contradiction in her classroom as she has allowed it to be run over the years:

> We vote about nearly everything in our democratic classrooms, but we permit the children to empower bosses and reject classmates. Just when the old-fashioned city bosses have all but disappeared and the once exclusive dining clubs are opening their doors to strangers, we still allow children to build domains of exclusivity in classrooms and playgrounds. (p. 22)

The label *rejected* is something children have to learn; being reject-ed in play foreshadows all the later rejections of life. "Of course," as Paley acknowledges, "the feeling begins much earlier, in life's first separations. We are so vulnerable once we are alone at school" (p. 27). But should children be left alone to figure out rejection for themselves? Is this the way we want to build a child's character in preparation for living in a rejecting world where wants and desires will often be frustrated?

As Paley's rule becomes inserted into the flow of behavior in the kindergarten class, it begins to conflict with the idea that someone should be in charge. Is it possible to rid ourselves of needing a boss? As one fourth-grade girl remarked, "Do away with owners and the rule could work" (p. 95). But this is hardly an easy task, when throughout society hierarchies are rigidly enforced. Take, for in-stance, the superhero dolls that my five-year-old nephew, Nicholas, plays with avidly, like so many others his age. On one of the pack-ages for Vipers, a member of the Cobra Infantry group, there appears a directive about starting at the bottom and gradually working one's way up the pyramid. And, for fighting intrepidly, those driven by cruelty and greed are rewarded by power and wealth.

Of course, kids don't read these messages, they just play the games. Yet the game is very much about where they fit in the verti-cal social structure and what kinds of adversarial urges they must have in order to climb the ladder over the bodies of others.

In short, the real opposition to Paley's plan stems from the gen-eral unfairness that exists in the world and the way children already imagine themselves preparing for future disappointments and rejec-tions. In a crucial exchange with some fifth graders, Paley uncovers this form of reasoning from one boy, "In your whole life you're not going to go through life never being excluded. So you may as well learn it now. Kids are going to get in the habit of thinking they're not going to be excluded so much and it isn't true." Paley responds, "Maybe our classes can be nicer than the outside world," but still the boy contends, "But this way you won't get down on yourself when you do get excluded." Nevertheless, Paley concludes, "Too often it's the same children, year after year, who bear the burden of rejection. They're made to feel like strangers." What she's come to understand is "that although we all begin school as strangers, some children never learn to feel at home, to feel they really belong. They are not made welcome enough" (pp. 100–103).

Able to stay with the children's objections, Paley talks openly about feelings and social relationships without being condescend-ing. Opinions are engaged directly in a caring way. The boy's conventional argument has long been an excuse for keeping people in their place, yet Paley boldly keeps asking the impossible. For instance, what if people actually expect to be treated properly by those in authority and get angry and protest when this doesn't happen? Following this boy's logic, discriminatory policies would never change, nor could we ever expect conditions to improve for marginalized groups.

Meanwhile, the magpie story has been progressing to a crisis point. The exploits and adventures of this bird have served as a continuous thread throughout Paley's account. Having himself been saved by a kindness, the magpie has gone on to share his kindness with others. Paley allows her *myth* to confront the feelings and behaviors engendered by acts of exclusion and to explore new scripts that turn the tables to everyone's satisfaction. The tale is about much more than getting along nicely with each other; it seeks a larger vision of what binds people together. The serial story of the magpie provides a way of emotionally, aesthetically, and ethically dramatizing the issues with which the children are struggling. In doing so, the story emphasizes how engagements with literature potentially foster democratic concerns and attitudes. For these children, this will not happen without Paley's direction, without her commitment to the dispersal of authority and her caring concern for expressed differences.

The final testing of the rule occurs during story acting, when children get to play out the parts in a story someone else has made up. This becomes a useful arena for acting out systematic favoritism and yet hiding it behind the reasonable request that all children ought to have the right to control their own stories and how they are presented to the group. And deeper dislocations also arise here, such as is it acceptable to invite a boy to play a girl? Yet having struggled with the rule for some time now, its presence in story acting frees the children to begin taking on

> implausible roles, shyly at the start, but after a while with great aplomb, as if accepting the challenge to eliminate their own stereotyped behaviors. Girls take on boy's roles and boys accept girl's roles. Not everyone, to be sure, but enough children are willing to throw off their shackles to make these role reversals acceptable. Those who have never taken roles as bad guys, witches, and monsters are saying yes to such assignments, and the Ninja Turtles are agreeing to be newborn babies. (p. 127)

Sheltered by the imaginative power of literature, these children were able to throw off the normal constraints of what was possible and so sympathetically take on the perspective of the other.

Paley understands that her achievement cannot be taken for granted. Indeed, only after a year-long campaign of gentle persuasion and consciousness raising do her children come to alter some of their original assumptions about what is acceptable interpersonal behavior. Where will they find such a rule practiced again once they leave her protective care? Still, her goal of moving her children beyond exclusion remains central to any democratic vision:

> We have our work cut out for us, in every grade, if we are to prepare children to live and work comfortably with the strangers that sojourneth among them. And should it happen that one day our children themselves are the strangers let them know that a full share of the sun is rightfully theirs. (pp. 129–30)

Unfortunately, as Paley realizes, the conduct that we learn at an early age often persists with us throughout our lives. All aspects of society contribute to the climate that makes certain "unacceptable" behaviors acceptable. If, for instance, governments can't show restraint, can we expect individual citizens to act any differently? A lack of concern for the conditions of human life at any one level affects attitudes at all levels. When violence predominates as a solution to conflict, or bigotry as a response to personal discomfort, the most insidious kinds of exclusion grow and prosper. Only by taking an early stand, as Paley shows, can we begin to question the deep-seated and supposedly innocent privilege and status that individuals try to construct for themselves at someone else's expense. Democracy shoulders every citizen with the responsibility of preventing any particular "advantage" from leaving us a nation of strangers.

Encouraging the Pleasures of Ironic Involvement

One central purpose of reading literature in a democracy with students of all ages is to give them space for their unique responses—everyone included. When responses are drawn out and shared in the midst of a democratic ethos, students learn to distinguish between the kind of authority that controls from positions of power and exclusion, and the kind of authority that influences from positions of reason and caring. By expressing rich forms of ambiguity, poems and stories offer a primary means for each person to learn how *point of view* or *perspective,* while initially supporting exclusion, eventually provides a basis for overcoming it.

All voices uttered from the vantage point of privilege in any hierarchy naturally want the existence of their perspective to remain invisible to others. People are supposed to remain tethered in their place, not develop and change. Reading literature can resist such stasis. In experiencing the tension of opposites expressed in myths, students can begin to appreciate the pleasures of irony and so have a basis for rejecting one-sided views. Ironic involvement—as opposed to the ironic detachment that isolates us from others—grows when we realize that we're inevitably bound to hold more than one position at once. Playing within communities of commitment and trust, we begin to acknowledge the relativity and intersubjectivity of our own perspectives. This cautions us against cynicism, which in due course only breeds self-exclusion.

Ironic involvement values connections. It sees across the gaps and contradictions that comprise our mutual desires. It tries to transcend the fragmentary and the antagonistic. It works at uncovering the paradoxical procedures of the institutions we've constructed to both realize and constrain caring relationships. But how can one replace confrontation, which by its nature seeks to exclude or silence someone, with conversations that develop ironic involvement?

One difficulty lies in the forms of competitive discourse primarily associated with males. When this preemptory way of talking prevails in classroom discussions of literature, power and control are at issue, not equal access. If the goal is to keep building toward mutuality, then, as teachers, we will reject winner-take-all approaches to whatever controversy arises. A caring rhetorical style provides an important way of refiguring how literary response talk might proceed. Such response talk would not render any participant silent. No one would have to yield to the dominant voice or voices in order to avoid the risk of ending up alone. Rather, everyone works to weave reciprocally dependent spaces that thrive on the riches of harmony and counterpoint—we fill in the score together. In this sense the connecting and noncompetitive aspects of what has been labeled woman's talk provide a script for how playful democrats might proceed when they engage with others in the work of response and interpretation. As Paley suggests, the discourse of inclusion serves to mediate what we previously allowed to divide us.

A discourse of inclusion reminds us that the measure of any reading event must finally reside in its satisfactions. For as Robertson Davies concludes, unless reading "brings pleasure first you should think carefully about why you are doing it" (Davies, p. 100). The pleasure of the text is more than the immediate thrill of appreciation or aesthetic gratification. Our reading pleasure comes from being aware of intentionality—that imaginative leap made by the mind as it recognizes correspondences between designs of coherence and closure in the text and internal body states of feeling and order. The satisfaction comes from a sense of "I get it!" and the savoring of the reverberations that arise from this. In responding to texts we too are given a voice, we too are included.

Pleasure indicates that the reader is holding the reins, not someone else, and so to teach literature democratically is not about the "correct" interpretation, but about fostering innovation—the endless novelty of new stories waiting to be told. Innovation always exists at the expense of authority; it's a kind of declaration of independence. The reading commitment most central to a democracy is the one that breaks a student's solitary dependence on the teacher. This includes everything from text selection to text meaning. Inquiring publicly into alternate readings, in order to distinguish those that are more satisfying from those that are less satisfying, can only take place after we feel pleasure in our own readings. This pleasure begins with being connected to our own knowledge and ends with some appreciation of the irony of another's contrary perspective.

Opening Texts That Find Us Out

I don't want to be threatened or unsettled any more than the next person, so why open my own story up to scrutiny in the classroom? One threatening episode in my quest to discover my identity as a teacher occurred in a class session being used to assess student accomplishments during an eight-week summer program. All students were supposed to prepare a presentation that in some way captured what they had learned and how they had gone about learning it. On the second day of presentations, I continued to sit silently, nodding approval, allowing Marlene, my coteacher, to be the one actively participating in the ongoing commentary with the students. In my mind, I was contemplating what form our teacher evaluation story might take, because, although publicly only the students had taken on this assignment, I too intended to make a presentation that captured how important the summer learning experience had been for the both of us as teachers.

Then suddenly, Chris, one of the students, addressed me before the entire group, "Well, are the instructors going to give assessment presentations too?" At that instant I felt blindsided, my feelings hurt. Why was I so angry and defensive? Why did I almost start sulking like a small child instead of responding in a light-hearted manner, "Yes, of course, and we can hardly wait!"? After all, I'd already begun planning what to say in our presentation. Yet, by some twisted logic, I felt that Chris should have known that; he should have known me. What authority gave me the right to expect students to be mind readers?

On reflection, it seems that the privilege and status from which my good intentions had sprung had been struck a near-fatal blow. How dare anyone think of questioning what I was going to do, let alone what I was silently feeling. Everyone should have taken for granted that I was naturally operating in good faith. Further, Chris's request prevented me from exhibiting an act of generosity, of displaying sensitivity from my place of authority. By having my good intentions preempted, I was accordingly diminished. Being called to account made me face a secret about myself. How inadequate I suddenly felt, inadequate at having been found out as less than perfect, as falling short. What a blow to my ego.

Because the sources of my privilege and status often remain invisible to me—from my WASP culture to my male gender—I was startled to discover how strongly I clung to the idea that only I was allowed to hold secrets, only I was allowed to exclude those around me by failing to disclose what I was feeling. Despite all my words to the contrary, it's hard to live in openness with students and not also expect instant allegiance from them. At least on this occasion, the shock caused me to reconsider my perspective. I needed to stop avoiding the risks of openness that I in turn was asking each student to take.

There is a widespread fear that openly questioning authority will ultimately lead to all values being viewed as radically contingent. Thus, one will no longer be able to promote the good or oppose the bad. The relativity of the teacher's perspective is supposed to contribute to this general moral decline. Barbara Herrnstein Smith, however, sees such relativity as a positive development: "acknowledging the fact and partiality of one's perspective" should not "in itself undermine someone's authority over her students, children, or native parishioners." In fact, such acknowledgment might make authority "more subject to interrogation" (Smith, p. 160). By contrasting one perspective with another, instead of presenting absolutes, the teacher displays a firm belief in democratic practice. Again, what is valued and respected is authority's reason, not its force. As Smith continues,

> the securing of authority from interrogation and risk could hardly be thought an unqualified or intrinsic good. On the contrary, it might be thought there was some communal value to ensuring that all authority was *always* subject to interrogation and *always* at risk. *All* authority: which must mean that of parent, teacher, and missionary as well as that of tyrant, pope, and state flunky. (p. 161)

Viewing authority in this way does not denigrate standards. When students claim ownership of their own texts, this does not isolate them from comparisons with the texts of others. It, in fact, encourages dialogue. Publicly owning their texts helps validate the students' own intentions and in turn establishes for them a significant zone of rebellion—one that can serve as the basis for committed and responsible action because it is never far from reason and reflection.

Authority must always be in decline, if the world is to go on living, to go on being born anew. The only thing the adult world can ever temper is the pace, the rate of transition. How I as a teacher meet students openly within the spaces of stories represents my particular contribution to their process of maturing. Giving up the old-style authority of the teacher, no longer remaining inscrutably in charge, keeping myself included in the present flow of classroom events—this will never be easy. Yet, might not the ironic pleasures of a text, brought alive in a democratic classroom, provide a testing ground, a kind of walkabout, for each student's emerging moral imagination? Might not literature allow students to grapple with a world buzzing with ideas and opinions not their own, buzzing with conclusions that deny those they've reached separately? By sharing and then relinquishing my ownership of poems and stories, how might I help create a social forum in which students' rebellious attitudes toward authority are critically voiced and fostered?

Chapter Six

Listening to Ourselves

Democratic conversations in the literature classroom begin with students listening to themselves. Responses to poems, we must remember, emanate from inside each reader. They do not come from what the reader is being told to think or feel. If, however, readers do not stand ready to hear these internal reactions, if they do not have ways of sanctioning the credibility of their own reactions, then talk about poems in the classroom becomes yet another round of hierarchical imposition. Thus, learning to read literature is, to a large extent, learning to listen to the responses that a text calls up in us. Still, this too is a social act. In listening to ourselves we come to remember how much we depend on our relationships with other selves.

Experiencing Words in the Body

Magically, it seems, much of our verbal power resides in potential bodily states. Our public utterances rely on an inner reservoir of immediate felt intentions. Thus, what we have to say is not the result of a script that is carefully rehearsed in advance. Rather, our words grow out of our lived experiences in the world (see Johnson, 1987). Sometimes our ability to access certain words even requires a specific setting. Recall is blocked unless the context is right. I remember, for instance, having a secret fear of forgetting the combination to my hall locker in high school. Whenever this fear came over me, I'd try to rehearse the sequence of numbers, but inevitably my mind would go blank. Yet when I stood in front of the locker, actually

engaged in spinning the cylinder with my fingers, the combination never deserted me. Somehow it existed as much in my hand as it did in my head.

Prior to entering the verbal world, infants experience a natural correspondence between their own bodily actions and the attuned responses of their caretaker. Out of this early, integrated wholeness, an infant gradually grows confidence in being able to represent the world with words, but this capacity for representation is inevitably tied to specific events. Infants that are *heard* learn that they will be able to negotiate new situations on their own. By associating their physical routines with interpersonal satisfactions, infants establish a foundation for relating the affective and cognitive aspects of language. In this way, knowledge is person connected, at least when an infant's primary need for nurturing has not been thwarted. Such integration leads us to speak of being in touch with our intuition. We know about the world through words that have been linked with bodily states, and this is what we feel when, in uttering some expression, we have the physical sensation of getting it right.

Yet many children are not encouraged to decipher the implications of their own words. They do not learn strategies for reflecting on their own self-expression. There seems to be a general fear of indwelling. Speech rushes madly onward, as if to overcome the seeming perils of awkward silences. Public fluency seems to overwhelm the hesitancy of conscious self-reflection. Unless we slow down and begin listening to ourselves, we have no way of being in touch with our assumptions about things and thus becoming answerable for the actions we are taking. Mindlessly filling the gaps of empty conversational space, fearing that we may be lost forever in its black hole, can be one way of avoiding listening to ourselves.

Students wanting direction, wanting to be told what to do, wanting help with the decisions they should be making, are most vulnerable to dependency. When I say, "Well, you tell me what you think your options are," and then I give the students time to breathe, not surprisingly, without too much prompting, a number of possibilities come pouring out. I can listen, in an open, nonjudgmental, Rogerian fashion, to what they are saying, attempting to uncover their implicit desires and not interrupt with my own. I can use my responses to note particular enthusiasms they may be expressing but have not yet detected themselves. A question or an idea can resonate back to the issues that have emerged in our previous conversations. They can be pushed to reword and thus reimagine what they are saying. This can allow them to recognize their

own deeper patterns of thought and concern. Encouraging such listening commits students to begin their own conversations.

This phenomenon of inner listening, of feeling the necessary correspondences between our words and our intentions, has been labeled by James Britton as "shaping at the point of utterance" (Britton, p. 139). Emphasizing how the process of shaping our language is socially driven, Britton suggests that, in listening to ourselves, we come up with expressions that we feel are right in terms of the verbal encounter we have been mutually constructing with our audience. The guiding and caring presence of others, real or imagined, helps to draw the words from us. Virtual conversations in our heads—when we act both as speaker and listener—are governed by the quality and quantity of our linguistic reserves, which in turn have been built up through the frequenting of texts, both spoken and written. The language with which one engages is internalized through reading and *being read to,* and gradually a stock is built up that one can draw on at the moment of need.

Applying this dynamic to writing, Britton concludes that "the developed writing process [is] one of hearing an inner voice dictating forms of the written language appropriate to the task at hand" (p. 144). Not to cultivate this inner resource through listening is to diminish greatly our integrative powers of self-expression. Only we as individuals know the nature of our relations with others, know the feeling of our intersubjective emotions, so inevitably it must be us who listen to what we know.

Forgetting What We Know

An alarming pattern of disintegration has come to light in women's stories. A particularly severe dilemma has been shown to exist when social conventions governing the world of personal relations clash with what women as individuals have previously found to be true. As a result, many women have been left with a diminished capacity to listen to the self. In *Meeting at the Crossroads,* Lyn Mikel Brown and Carol Gilligan offer a devastating commentary on the state of listening in our culture. Reporting on a five-year-long study, in which the lives of 100 girls were investigated, Brown and Gilligan reveal how girls choose to become less intelligent by denying the knowledge of human feelings and relationships that was quite clear to them before they entered adolescence. Interviewed yearly, some from age eight to thirteen, others from age twelve to seventeen, these girls offer stories of the struggle they face in trying to keep alive their bodily sense of knowledge. Many find it hard to resist the barrage of influences that seek to censor what a girl knows in return for her fitting peacefully within existing affiliations.

Wanting to avoid being the outsider, girls begin to ward off their own insights. The language they use to present themselves often grows vague and uncertain. Judy, for example, at thirteen can still see that people ought to talk openly about their differences when they're in a conflict situation. Yet because such an exposure of potentially disagreeable thoughts and feelings might threaten her comfortable membership in the group, she caves in, rejecting as a viable option such speaking out. Struggling to remain self-connected, Judy is already aware that a child's ability to listen internally is inexorably snuffed out by the culture—"you just sort of forget your mind" (Brown and Gilligan, p. 138).

> Like little babies, they can't understand . . . they have . . . really nothing, because they're just starting, but then . . . by like seven . . . they have the most mind, but they are starting to lose it actually. . . . [Given] what you learn in school . . . [what's] shoved at you into your brain, people seem to just like sort of gradually forget about that and then just worry about the sums and totals of checks and stuff, and it is sort of stagnant . . . I mean, it's sort of just like they have other things on their mind and they don't want to worry about [the feeling] . . . or maybe perhaps that since they don't know what it is, they don't want to have to worry about it. (p. 138)

When adults no longer listen to the self, feelings are separated from actions. This, however, is not the case with Judy. With a wonderful sense of symmetry she brings her understanding of development back to its beginnings as she imagines how the listening cycle is completed in old age:

> When you start to realize that you are going to be dying soon, I think that perhaps then some people start to get it back, because they are sort of sick and tired of all that brain stuff . . . maybe that's why grandparents get along so good with grandchildren, because they're really old and they're really young and they sort of connect. (p. 138)

Despite these sensitivities, Judy, like the other girls, experiences the loss of resiliency during adolescence. This brittleness of selfhood might be traced to a significant failure of the listening environment. In the conversational encounters convened by adults, insufficient attention is given to how conflict and oppositional ("bad") feelings might be engaged, rather than avoided. The lesson is clear: Fitting in, not rocking the boat, means you stop listening and live outwardly on the surface of things.

To stay in relationships as they are conventionally defined in society, girls must appear innocent, must render themselves oblivious to their knowledge of relationship. This causes their initial, outwardly directed, political resistance to be transformed into an inwardly directed, psychological resistance—a transformation that often haunts their adult relationships and cripples their agency in the world. When they stop listening to themselves, these girls also stop pressuring the social system. They know this system is unfair because it won't acknowledge their contradictory feelings, the sadness and anger in their voices. Adults don't listen to these girls, however, preferring to avoid talk about unpleasant feelings. And so younger girls find themselves with nowhere to turn when their feelings need expression in open and frank discussion. Instead, they learn to put aside their original powers of listening.

On one occasion, Gilligan and her colleagues took a group of eleven-year-old girls from the Boston area on a week-long retreat. There the girls wrote and did drama work that helped them function as a group and talk about subjects they wouldn't ordinarily discuss in order to speak their voices in public. As one colleague relates it: "The kids had to direct and listen to one another, they wrote some beautiful pieces and did some really interesting drawings and formed a community among themselves" (Prose, p. 46). Relieved of normal social pressures, and launched into imaginative but safe zones of creative dramatics, these young girls were able to express concerns about their social world that otherwise are generally silenced.

Yet when girls from the ages of eight to twelve do speak up with their knowledge of fairness and relationship, how are they heard? Unfortunately, adults, both men and women, frequently find it easier to consider them "disturbed," rather than allow their wisdom to be taken in and used to "disturb" an otherwise unjust system, one set up to privilege power, competition, and separation—ways of being often associated with males. Reading an unedited version of Anne Frank's diary, Gilligan discovered three kinds of passages that were either deliberately or unconsciously censored out by her father.[1] Each passage connected to the threatening knowledge that girls possess before having to deny it: 1. Knowledge of the body: Anne tells of discovering her body and its sexuality. 2. Knowledge of the contradictions of relationship: Anne complains that her mother is not showing her useful ways of being an adult and also reveals a deep tension in their relationship. 3. Knowledge about unfairness in a world that treats women in subordinate ways: Anne pleads for justice and opportunity for women in a manner as fresh and determined as any feminist writing today.

Surely a society that is male dominated has some purpose in systematically suppressing such understandings in young girls. Accordingly, it's not surprising that literature and art, as major repositories of this knowledge, are mostly rendered subordinate in education. It seems literary response can end up raising too many questions. The girls' early plea for a way of airing conflict and disagreement represents a direct commitment to democratic processes, but the risk of exposure that democracy encourages is often too great to bear.

When listening to self is not valued in the literature classroom, student readers end up at cross-purposes. In reading a poem, they can come into conflict with *self* if they refuse to be in conflict with the response of the prevailing authority. In contrast to this, Brown and Gilligan tell of a resistant reading a girl gave to Andrew Marvell's poem "To His Coy Mistress." Responding from the perspective of the woman being addressed in the poem, Anjli reversed the teacher-sanctioned reading and, feeling its violation, "called the poem morbid and found it terrifying and chilling" (Brown and Gilligan, p. 223). Against the judgments of other teachers, Anjli's teacher stuck with her and respected her challenge to the standards, thereby opening up a new appreciation of the poem's power. Yet at the same time that her painful interpretation was being valued and not forced underground, Anjli came to understand the "accepted" reading and on what occasions she would be required to parrot it for less-sympathetic examiners. This is the lesson learned by too many students, that acting intelligently and being a "good" student usually represent divergent paths. Thus they work hard at playing the game of school, instead of being fearless seekers after learning and knowledge.

This is the crucial insight and invitation Brown and Gilligan provide. Teachers need to re-examine channels of communication in their classrooms, stay with feelings, and not be so ready to pave over unpleasantness. One teacher, for example, heeding this new way of being with girls, "found herself permitting a loud personal argument in her classroom and was astonished to be thanked by the two girls for not interrupting them" (Brown and Gilligan, p. 222). In a second instance, this teacher "resisted her impulse to close off an emotionally tense conflict over a heated political question. She had come to see confronting conflict openly with strong feelings in public as essential to young women's education" (p. 222). How will we encourage these missing voices in our own classrooms? How will we demonstrate that it is alright for students to listen to themselves and become committed to their individual responses? How will we model for students democratic procedures for questioning, examining, and revising thoughts and feelings in concert with others? Can we find ways of welcoming controversy and contention so that a girl's knowledge can stay with her? Need silence be the price paid for inclusion?

Note

1. Gilligan lecture at the Harvard Club, New York City, 19 May 1992.

Chapter Seven

The World from Another Perspective

As teachers, we too have selves and histories that must be heard. If we want to appreciate the contrary responses and perspectives that students inevitably bring to our classrooms, it will be helpful to draw on our own lessons of discrepancy. This involves recalling those moments in our educational past when our thinking was out of line, when our point of view was not officially sanctioned. Then we might pay close attention to ourselves feeling what the outsider feels. In this way, we sympathetically begin to imagine the difficult work that democratic conversations require if all voices are to be welcomed.

What most galvanized my sense that perspective could never be solitary or monolithic occurred when I was a junior in high school and we were studying the American Revolution—the War of Independence. This originating moment in our history appeared to grow out of a clear-cut ideological struggle, one that brought out the kind of bravery, determination, and resiliency that allows truth to triumph over greatly superior forces. Regardless of how the moment is analyzed—Was taxation without representation the crucial issue or was it opportunism on the part of propertied patricians?—the American Revolution has proven to be a crucial shot heard round the world, a watershed for democracy and self-determination.

The teaching question when it comes to such subject matter is how much ambiguity of fact and interpretation should be allowed. Presumably, students should believe in the ideals of America and feel proud of their citizenship, so teachers don't want to keep carping at every fault or imperfection uncovered in historical events. The challenge is how to create in students a sensibility that is critically aware of the contradictions of history, of people's conflicting motives and actions, and yet does not leave them feeling disillusioned and despairing. Nice pluralistic sentiments, but pressing these lessons home is another matter, even when the teacher believes them.

In her most recent book, *Human Minds,* Margaret Donaldson describes a major developmental change in children that occurs around the age of nine: Transcendent modes begin to characterize a child's outlook. Detachment is now possible because the other's perspective can be entertained. Children can begin to be concerned with ideas and people on their own terms and not merely as extensions of their own desires or intentions. Well, at 16 years old I was long past the age of being ready to take in the other's point of view. School, however, tends to ignore genuine debate, especially when the myths of the defining culture risk being contradicted. Tangling with perspective often involves uncovering some profound tension between reason and loyalty. The consequence of seeing it one way rather than another amounts to affirming one's particular group membership. In the case of studying the American Revolution, one might complicate all the issues, show any number of imperfections and mixed motives, but in the end it's always one side pitted against the other. While it's entirely possible to appreciate the point of view of each of the contenders, it's difficult to be an American and not clearly see the rebel cause as just. But that's precisely the reversal of experience in which I was so instructively caught.

Our teacher, Mr. Symmes, was open minded as he sought to have students explore the conflicting reasons—many of them less than noble—for this armed insurrection against the Crown. Freedom, liberty, self-determination, and economic opportunity, however, were significant, unifying themes, and this strong American ethos was positively reinforced by my father. He certainly believed in the American dream, having proven that one could be born of immigrant parents who lived in a slum and then rise, through education and hard work, to the comforts of the middle class.

The year before I was to study the grand event in school, my father bought me a copy of *The American Heritage Book of The Revolution*—its dust jacket boasting a brilliantly colored painting of American troops triumphantly planting an American flag on a battlefield amid wounded and dying redcoats. I was primed and ready to read about the strategies and sacrifices that made it possible for America to sever its ties with England and launch the course of its own national destiny. In the introduction, however, the acclaimed historian Bruce Catton provided a small note of caution. The American

Revolution was, of course, fought by "living, aspiring, struggling people" just like the rest of us, but a "romantic haze has settled down over the whole affair" making it difficult to remember how much the war "was a hard, wearing, bloody, and tragic business—a struggle to the death that we came very close to losing" (Lancaster, p. 6). Like today, the people at that time "were often confused, usually divided in sentiments, and now and then rather badly discouraged about the possible outcome of the tremendous task they had undertaken" (p. 6). Indeed, as Catton confessed, there were two discernable sides to this struggle, "no more than a third of the provincials were active patriots . . . another third were Loyalists, with the remaining third uncommitted" (p. 6). Yet in the end, the crucial fact was that enough people "were willing to fight and die for what they believed in to make the dream of independence and freedom come true" (p. 6). Because Catton was rightfully proud to be an American, he was deeply invested in Americans venerating this special moment in their history: "we who look back at them owe them a debt whose size is almost beyond our comprehension" (p. 7).

What followed from this attempt to open the volume in an even-handed manner was a stirring rendition of the intricate details of the entire campaign—from the brink of defeat in New York to victory at Yorktown. But decidedly it was a tale told from the perspective of the winning side. Indeed, no longer was there any mention of Loyalists or the agony of choosing sides. Instead, the foreign enemy came into focus and the label quickly turned into those dreaded Tories. History continued to be the story of the victors.

I was perfectly willing to go along with all this; still, another voice kept beckoning from the wings. Also sitting on our shelf at home was another massive volume—well over eight hundred pages—but this was a historical novel. Facing the title page were these words taken from Edward Floyd DeLancey's introduction to Jones' *History of New York*:

> In 1821, Chief Justice John Jay said to his nephew William Heathcote DeLancey: "Let me tell you, William: the *true* history of the American Revolution can *never* be written." Jay declined to give his reasons, saying, "You must be content to know that the fact is as I have said, and that a great many people in those days were not at all what they seemed, nor what they are generally believed to have been."

The first-person narrative that followed, *Oliver Wiswell* by Kenneth Roberts, brought me back to the other half of my roots, for it unwaveringly revealed the complex perspective of those who happened to be on the "wrong" side during the War for Independence. Drawn in emotionally by the injustices and hardships faced by the Loyalists at the hands of the rebels, it was time to awaken my Canadian heritage that I had inherited through my mother. And so at last I came to sympathize with what my forebears must have suffered as they were forced to leave New York and New England, and resettle in the Maritime Provinces. That war may have been long over and enmities long forgotten, but it was important to discover a different essence of what once had been—my forebears were not Tories, but United Empire Loyalists.

Roberts' fiction powerfully imparted this other awareness. True, my consciousness of my Canadian ancestry stood waiting below the surface to link up with the story of Oliver Wiswell, but Canadian memory had always been held in measured refrains. There was nothing pugnacious or adversarial about Canada's alternative view of the world, for Canadians, I naively supposed, remain conspicuously unjingoistic—forgive and forget. Let a reserved calm and politeness guide human conduct. It was more prudent to let peace prevail over discord. Indeed, many social commentators have noted the Canadian temperament of quietism. While the United States promises *just* government, Canada simply offers up *good* government. The difference can be fundamental, with an emphasis on mediation and negotiation replacing fractious confrontation. In fact, among relatives on the Canadian side of my family, the main contention I remember being expressed—except for my mother's outrage and disgust at how immigration officials had treated her when our family moved to the States—was an irritation over the fact that the Americans had entered the second World War two whole years after the Canadians and then demanded all the bragging rights. Perhaps this was only the tip of the iceberg in a series of slights and complaints.

During eight years of trials and tribulations, in which he travels through many of the colonies in service of the loyalist cause, Oliver Wiswell tells a complex adventure that spares no idiocy, duplicity, or atrocity on either side of the conflict. War is "a consuming fever: a period of delirium and insanity, of misery, disappointment, discomfort, anxiety, despair, waste, weariness, boredom, brutality, death" (Roberts, p. 291). This is no romanticized version of the conflict, for each man "forgets, if he ever knew, the principles for which he's fighting, and they seldom enter his mind except when he hears them mouthed by politicians who have never under any circumstances faced enemy bullets and would never endure the daily discomforts of a soldier" (p. 434).

As the fortunes of the Loyalists decline, Oliver vents openly to a friend the accumulated anger and bitterness that he feels toward the rebels:

> They're the people who boast of being American patriots, and brand you and me as traitors to our country. We're loyal, and so we're traitors. They break their words, dishonor their treaties, make war on women, oppress the weak and helpless, practise the worst sort of political oppression, and so they're patriots! It rips me to pieces inside to see such men take our country from us! (p. 531)

Seeing the Loyalist perspective expressed repeatedly in reaction to fictionally recreated historical episodes had a cumulative effect on me. I experienced a shift in reality. The rebels' wartime rhetoric of freedom and independence came to have a hollow ring to it—or at least serious doubts came into my mind about conventional patriotism. For this was not just another intellectual exercise of imagining different angles of vision. Here I saw that a whole people, to whom I was inevitably connected, had in fact read the events of the American Revolution quite differently than I had been led to suppose.

Every icon of the period could be viewed in a sordid light. I read, for instance, "never has there been a more adroit and unscrupulous government agent than Benjamin Franklin, or a more harmless-seeming one." Franklin "delighted in forging letters, full of barefaced lies and foul hints, that destroyed the character and reputation of anyone antagonistic to the rebel cause" (p. 483). Then there was Lafayette described as a "little boy, Washington's pet." Washington, I learned, turned "to putty" whenever Lafayette asked for anything: "That little French boy's no more fit to be a general and plan a battle than a baby is" (p. 758). And what a difference to discover that Benedict Arnold was a hero, not a traitor, because he finally saw the light and joined the loyalist cause. Nothing was sacred once I started to read with another lens.

Finally, in 1783, Oliver ends up safely in New Brunswick, Canada. In this last section of the novel, ambiguously entitled "Land of Liberty" (America lost, Canada gained?), our understanding is directed toward peacefully accommodating the results of the war. Oliver's concluding words foreshadow the future: "Perhaps something great will come out of all that agony and all those deaths, all that intolerance and all that cruelty. Perhaps something great will come even to that rabble some day, as well as to us" (p. 836). With hostilities ended, it was time to regain some sense of harmony, to see similarity rather than difference. For, despite this alternate perspective on the war, losing gave no one the right to go on clinging to some deep-seated grudge. Reading these events from a new perspective stirred my sense of identity; it did not evoke any hatred for grievances suffered at the hands of a long-ago enemy.

In reimagining the significance of this incident to my education, I again took *Oliver Wiswell* off the shelf and discovered the note card that I had used to organize the oral presentation about the novel that I gave to my junior-year history class. At the top of the card, I'd written: "About revolution, but new/different slant on it." I then sketched an outline of the main events of the story and focused on Oliver's negative perception of war, before concluding with the words "excellent book—would not recommend."

The reason not to recommend? Perhaps, already, I was divided on how far a person's perspective might be shifted if they weren't somewhat predisposed, for there at the end of the card I had repeated the initial note to myself: "(different slant on Rev.)." Somehow I realized the advantages of cautiously obscuring my presence as outsider in order not to risk displaying myself too far apart: Would anyone else in the class really understand that a historical perspective might be this radically different? And also correct? It seemed too much to ask others to imagine my alternative, foreign identity as actually being connected to this sacred moment in *our* past. There, the *we* was once again in place, and I could return these newly charged feelings back into the safe confines of my mind.

But this knowledge could never really be erased. A very specific loyalist story has survived in my family's papers and a ceremonial sword that I have now inherited provides a most tangible link to this alternative perspective. The sword originally belonged to Captain Thomas Spragg, my great-great-great-great grandfather, who served in the French and Indian War. In 1783, at age 53, Thomas Spragg (Sprague) was forced to flee Hempstead, Long Island, and resettle his family in New Brunswick, Canada. One letter in particular describes this event:

> [He] was found among the leading Loyalists at the time of the revolution—holding a commission in the local forces—coming from Long Island. He survived the battles, and when the revolutionists were victorious, returned to his homestead, where he hoped he would be permitted to carry on quietly under the new form of government.
>
> The Americans apparently would not overlook his loyalist activities, and marked him down as deserving the worst they were handing out. It was autumn, and the gathering of the corn. The Captain was in his barn storing the corn, while his men gathering it from the adjoining field, carried it in large baskets on their head,

to dump it at their master's feet in the barn. When one of the men brought in his basket, he reported a body of American soldiers converging on the place, in fact with his load he had passed safely through their lines. The Captain knew of course the soldiers' purpose—his capture. The workman suggested that the Capt. exchange clothes with him, turn the basket upside-down, which was the custom, and walk back to the field, which now lay back of the lines, and perhaps escape. The exchange was quickly made, the basket turned over the Captain's head, and he walked quietly out, passed through the lines, and reached the woods. How he had done so, they did not know, nor where to look for him they did not know, and the workmen were loyally silent. The property was seized, and the family became the charges of the government. So far as the Captain was concerned, all was lost.

Our ancestor safely reached the coast, managed to get passage on a vessel and in time reached Saint John, what was then Nova Scotia, Canada. When in Saint John, he made application for compensation, for his loyalty and his losses for the same. So came the Spragg Grant. He took a canoe and alone found his way to his new property. It is said, that on reaching his grant, he erected a bark lean-to, and as night settled on him, he lay down under his bark roofing. It was then raining, and he said, "At last I am again on my own property, under the flag of my King, and at peace." And he said, "I went off peacefully to sleep."

Banishment, escape, adventure, resiliency, solitude, triumph. What additional male stories, now long since lost, chronicled the other names I've found inserted on the family tree: Morrell, Clarke, Slipp, VanWart, Merritt, Peters, Ryson, Corey, Tilley, Haines, Birdsell, Davis, Lamoreaux, Mercereau, Southard, Gritman, Carman, Harding, Crawford, Case, Drake, Marsters, O'Dell, Gillis, McDonald. Constantly, in my family papers, I read this refrain of separation: "The family was divided during the American Revolution with the majority favoring the Republic; others fought for the Crown and were banished at the close of hostilities." And I see a pattern of persecution and flight being indicated in these records: The Morrell (Morel) family were supposedly "descendants of Huguenots who had to flee France after the revocation of the Edict of Nantes in 1685 and went to England." A Dr. John Clarke was arrested for religious fanaticism and ideas, "severely beaten with many lashes, blood streaming from the wounds, then imprisoned and threatened with the gallows," before finally being banished from Boston to Rhode Island.

Belief, loyalty, perspective—all must be negotiated if our other selves are to gain a voice and become part of the alternative narratives of history. Democracy allows for, and then celebrates, origins that were not initially respectable—national, ethnic, institutional, personal. People can exist outside the master narrative. Conceding, but not surrendering to, all the gaps and conflicts that emerge as we search out our origins, we learn to exploit the possibilities of pluralism. The ultimate promise in our democracy is that alternate routes of arrival will hold no special advantage for any group or individual.

Reading Roberts' work of fiction touched me deeply, as it allowed my hidden ancestry to reach up and proclaim me as *other*. Having experienced this shock of awareness, I could hardly turn around—when fully inscribed as insider—and exclude any other. Even in high school I was suddenly able to look around and see groups of students who were being treated differently from me, who were being excluded from my privileged academic program for reasons other than intelligence. How did they feel?

Who could have imagined the salutary effect this rebellion against the Crown would have on my understanding the importance of being able to navigate the perilous shoals of truth and perspective. It was not just an intellectual lesson; my feelings had been deeply engaged through this reading experience with a text no one would claim as great literature. How did revealing my response risk labeling me as a foreigner? Was I learning less about the American Revolution and more about what it means to be on the outside of the lesson?

Chapter Eight

The Teacher as Listener

Children's comments often reveal classrooms in which rules and order prevail. Ironically, these regulations are justified as creating the necessary climate for learning. Instead, they all too easily provide a cover for not listening to students. What might we hear if we eavesdropped for a moment:

> Teachers are always saying, "Finish the question you are on." The reason I really hate this is that I've been stuck on the question for ten minutes, and I don't know the answer.

> They say "Shut up!" when they are the only ones talking—usually about the "noise level in this room." Then there's "I'm not repeating myself." But what do they do? Yes, you've guessed it.

> Teachers say: Shut up! Sit up! Clear up that mess! Do you do that at home! Do you want to do the teaching? Come to the front and read this! Go to the headmaster!!! Or they just: Glare!!! Point!!! Clear their throat!!! Slam rulers down!!!—We just secretly say "No!"

When students are allowed to speak, their complaints even go beyond the confines of the classroom: "Some grown-ups think children don't say anything important . . . so they don't listen." Early on, children learn to read the deeper intentions of adult behavior: "Find your own place and leave me alone." As another child commented, "In the garage: Dad? Yes? Can I help? No. Please? No. Oh. If you want to help go and tidy your bedroom. (He means, 'Get out of my way.')"[1]

In exploring the kind of talking that teachers encourage with young children, Christine O'Hanlon was surprised to find how hard it is for teachers to avoid speaking down to young children. It seems "there is little reciprocation or equal sharing of experience and fun between the adult and the child, as there would be between one child and another" (O'Hanlon, p. 56). For example, in this exchange with a six-year-old, in the midst of a "conversation" about going to the dentist, the teacher cannot drop the role of interrogator:

> **Teacher:** Oh! It made your teeth all squeaky?
> **B:** Un-huh (laughs).
> **Teacher:** Did you feel it?
> **B:** Eh? What? (screws up her face and widens her eyes).
> **Teacher:** The squeakiness, did you feel his rubber gloves rubbing against your teeth?
> **B:** mmm . . . felt all rubbery and plastic (laughs). (p. 54)

As they talk back and forth, it's the child who speaks in the fullest utterances and who is generally responsible for initiating and expanding the vocabulary being used, "introducing words like packaging, injection, mask and breathing" (p. 53). O'Hanlon acknowledges that "teacher's questioning is an important means of extending children's thinking at appropriate times," but she also wonders why "teachers believe that a conversation involves adults questioning without equal contribution from participants . . . Do teachers really ever *converse* with children?" (p. 54). In short it appears "that children are learning NOT how to talk from teacher but how to question, interrupt and test out their knowledge in encounters with adults" (p. 54).

As teachers one of our greatest fears is losing control of the classroom. Thus it's easier to speak and question rather than listen. For if we listen, we think that students will just talk about their own interests and leave the lesson behind. Already there are too many agendas spinning in the air to get anything done. The pressure to keep the lid on is great. Indeed, for every student who wants to talk more, one will want us to keep authority firmly in place. As one beginning tenth-grade teacher, who was trying to create a more open classroom, expressed the problem:

> My dilemma is that I feel as if I am not being seen as an effective teacher (by the students) unless I kowtow to the "commonsense" way of teaching, telling them what to learn. It is true that only two or three students have voiced such opinions, but it is a consistent voice that repeats itself in my head. Should I simply ignore these two students or should I take their advice to see what happens? How can I make them aware that they are learning as we discuss different issues in class, even though they might not be able to actually see on paper what they have learned? They don't seem comfortable when taking learning into their own hands, how can I help them to be more comfortable and to trust their own opinions rather

than just mine? How can I get them to see that this is what learning is about? (personal conversation)

Have these students already learned their lesson too well, that they
have nothing important to say because earlier no one respected
them by listening? In a survey by Sharon Wieland of 49 students
aged seven to fourteen, the vast majority reported that discussion
could only be forwarded by the teacher, and in fact no one realized
that "discussions might take place among a group of students without the teacher present" (Wieland, p. 2). So this is the lesson teachers cumulatively convey: "Somewhere along the way students learn
that their teachers want and expect a rigid, controlled environment
in the classroom" (p. 3).

Many teachers, however, are trying out new routines, despite
some initial loss of face. Barbara Canterford, a teacher in Australia,
describes a literature discussion group she ran during thirty-three
half-hour sessions with eight children from grade six. Attempting to
encourage the open reading responses of these students, Canterford
soon discovered that some of her traditional authority would have
to be relinquished. Moving toward her new role of participant/facil-
itator did not, however, mean that she had any less control than in
her previous role. What was important was that role relations needed to be explicitly reconstituted:

> The difference between the two roles lay in the social relations
> that developed with the group involved in the discussion. The
> children had to develop a different view of me as the teacher and
> of the way that learning took place. The mutual recognition of the
> value of sharing, which applied to me as much as to the children,
> contributed to this development. (Canterford, p. 287)

Just like Sharon Wieland, this teacher realized that students would
not talk democratically unless they were deliberately encouraged to
do so through her own commitment to acting differently in the
classroom and changing the power relationships involved in learning. This included making time for self-reflective conversation
about how everyone was conversing and why.

To practice a selfless kind of listening is not to be sheared of
identity or authority; it's not to be drowned in the outpourings of
students. In fact, active listening suggests a strongly composed
sense of self. In touch with our own selves, we can appreciate the
effects of intrusion and how our adult egos constantly risk swamp-
ing the egos of the young. There's a children's story called *The Other Way to Listen* about an old man from the hills who "was so good
at listening—once he heard wildflower seeds burst open, beginning

to grow underground" (Baylor and Parhall, p. 3). Eventually, this old man, "who could walk by any corn field and hear the corn singing" (p. 9), reveals the crucial attitude behind his listening. "Well, you have to respect that tree or hill or whatever it is you're with. Take a horned toad, for example. If you think you're *better* than a horned toad you'll never hear its voice—even if you sit there in the sun forever" (p. 17). Following this example, we might act on our human capacity to center our listening on relationship.

The Role of Constructs in Listening

The teacher as listener provides a transitional space for the learner to move between one mental representation of the world and another. In one sense the basic listening issue reduces to this: how a person's mental system of representing the world is subject to influence and change. One psychological model that helps us think about this question is found in the work of George Kelly. The fundamental postulate of Kelly's theory of personal constructs asserts: "A person's processes are psychologically channelized by the ways in which he anticipates events" (Kelly, p. 46). Because each of us carries around in his or her head a series of *constructs* (what we might call interpretive lenses, maps, or scripts) that allows us to predict social events, the way *role* and *relationship* are constructed in the classroom helps determine how a teacher's listening will contribute to a student's learning.

Mental constructs, which govern both perception and conception, generally work smoothly because they are largely invisible to our conscious awareness or attention. Only through some breakdown in the system—what we sometimes label *mistakes* or *errors* when we get a response that we hadn't expected—do we realize how powerfully determinant are the theories we carry around in our heads. Max Wertheimer tells the story of an anthropologist who was working on the grammar of a native language. On one particular occasion, his informant was unable to translate a certain sentence. "Puzzled, he tried to find out what words or grammatical inflections might be causing the trouble. It was only after some time that the native burst out, 'How can I translate this sentence of yours: "The white man shot six bears today"? This is nonsense. It is impossible that the white man could shoot six bears in one day!'" (Wertheimer, p. 274). Failing to share the anthropologist's point of view that words need not match actual conditions in the world, the informant had to cease his translating.

That constructs constrict understanding and behavior is an important theme in literature. Frequently a central character is so locked into a particular perspective that all evidence to the contrary is blocked out. The narrative thus either slowly proceeds to "enlighten" this entrenched bias or proceeds to show the consequences, often tragic, of a closed mind. Elizabeth Bennet, in Jane Austen's *Pride and Prejudice,* is but one example of a character who grows beyond her prejudice. Gradually, she comes to recognize her true feelings for Fitzwilliam Darcy, but the plot works reciprocally, for he in turn has had to temper his own pride because of his growing love for Elizabeth.

Despite the control our theories of the world exert over our understanding and our behavior, these theories are subject to modification when they are exposed to the continual give and take of social relations. This dialectic of resistance and change constitutes the arena in which listening occurs. If the venture of listening is to be beneficial, there must be *some mutual acceptance of the other's point of view.* As Kelly explains, "the person who is to play a constructive role in a social process with another person need not so much construe things as the other person does as he must effectively construe the other person's outlook" (Kelly, vol. 1, p. 95).

Creating a Facilitative Social Script

We demonstrate mutuality when we acknowledge that students have much to tell us. Sharing some of my own writing with students has shown me that such trust can awaken confidence in the learner. One student explained it this way:

> I think of the times you have asked me to respond to what you have written, starting with the Robert Coles review, where I felt *unequal*— and yet the gesture on your part was one that assumed equality. Each time you have asked me to respond to a piece of writing, the relationship between equality and inequality seemed closer. In my ability to respond to the present text, the relationship feels mutual. I trust myself in my response, knowing that it is part of a dialogue— and I trust that you will ask me questions to continue the dialogue. Anyway, it was important that you asked me to respond in the beginning even though I felt inadequate to the task. It is all change over time—the narrative principle. (personal communication)

Naively, I had assumed we were working together as equals from the start. I'd forgotten the inherent disadvantages students frequently feel when they first slip into the academic conversation. Still, eventually, without calculation, there developed an equality of response and listening between this student and myself.

What I seek to develop for myself as a teacher-listener is a kind of facilitating social script, one that embodies the values of reflective listening. Such facilitation supports and encourages as it draws the learner forth. The challenge is to listen with absorbed amazement, establishing context and connection. Yet in attempting to listen caringly, it may be awhile before we can incorporate the referents of the other into our own view of the world. As a teacher trying to listen to the concerns of my students, I constantly struggle to find ways of preventing my helping from intruding on the learner's own autonomy and agency. If, as a teacher, I wish to serve as a listener in order to draw out and explore each learner's evolving representations of the world, I will have to be patient and try to get straight just what each learner first understands.

Teachers who would foster a student's reading competence grasp the importance of their self-less role. We need to be secure enough in our obvious dominion over the learner to place our own fears and ambitions aside and wait to receive the inquiries of students—being with them, but not possessing them. This is one of the difficult dilemmas in my own teaching: How do I play a meaningful role both within and outside of the *relationship* that the student (as "knower") is constructing with the curriculum (as "known")? The challenge resides neither in my relationship with the subject matter nor in my relationship with the student. Rather, my focal awareness needs to be directed at my relationship with this *relationship*. I try to enter in the middle of the student-subject continuum and not get trapped at either end. For what I would teach students does not exist free of their intentional connection to it. Indeed, as we are now discovering, this knowing relationship—between a sense of self and a sense of an impinging world made up of objects, operations, and others—characterizes learning even in the youngest of infants. Until we wake up to the complex interpersonal relationships implied in listening, there is little chance of us becoming contingent to the responses students are struggling with as we try to read literature together.

Listening to the learner means I am striving toward an interpersonal role relationship that might be described as *mature dependency*. Infants, because they are unable to survive without their mothers, determine the immature end of the dependency continuum. At its opposite is not independence, but rather the kind of relationship that is possible between friends, lovers, learners, workers, a wife and husband. Each involves reciprocal dependency, which defines maturity (a social concept) as opposed to self-sufficiency (an individual concept). Facilitative listening allows for the reciprocity that makes mature dependency possible—the capacity to play a social role in relation to someone else, while allowing others to play a role in relation to you. In this way listening is not merely a route to learning, it is learning itself.

Keeping ourselves within the circle of listening, as Roland Barthes suggests, is the only way we can break out of the traditional patterns of authority we have inherited:

> Traditional societies knew two modes of listening, both alienated: the arrogant listening of a superior, the servile listening of an inferior (or of their substitutes); today this paradigm is contested, still crudely, it is true, and perhaps inadequately: it is believed that, in order to liberate listening, it suffices to begin speaking oneself—whereas a free listening is essentially a listening which circulates, which permutates, which disaggregates, by its mobility, the fixed network of the roles of speech: it is not possible to imagine a free society, if we agree in advance to preserve within it the old modes of listening: those of the believer, the disciple, and the patient. (Barthes, p. 259)

When no one listens to children, their initial burst of power and confidence with language inevitably withers. Thus, there can be no escaping, in a democracy, the central role the teacher as listener plays in the education of the young. At stake is the kind of listeners they will become.

Teachers Listening to Each Other

Growing as listeners, we learn to reconfigure our dominion as teachers. The struggle to create reciprocity with the learner seems endless. Indeed, our responsibility as teacher-listener never stops. There will always be one more story waiting to be told by a student and one more story we need to tell. Deciphering its intent, not merely applying a quick label, requires a great deal of energy and a great deal of restraint. For after awhile our alertness fails, having to contend endlessly with growing selves vying for attention. Will we come to acknowledge the sheer drain, the personal costs extracted from the listener? How might we create spaces within our professional communities where, in turn, we as teachers will experience others who reflectively listen to us, to our stories, to our real concerns? How might we affirm that our teaching pleasures exist within some shared territory of our stories? Will we eventually realize that, in making time for another teacher, we are really learning to listen to ourselves?

Note

1. Each child's comment in this paragraph appeared in the handout "Are you listening out there?" (Great Britain: National Oracy Project). This group has put out a number of materials that encourage teachers to reexamine their practices through the nudge of irony, such as "50 Successful Ways for Making Children Not Learn Through Talk": no choice of activity, encourage competitiveness, nothing on the walls, no interruptions, belittle spoken ideas, etc.

Chapter Nine

Literature and Exploration

Listening to the other person is difficult when social relationships are predominantly defined in hierarchical terms, when they depend on vertical rather than horizontal arrangements among citizens. Yet, when respectful listening prevails in a classroom, open conversations about literature can begin. Such conversations explore the social implications of the range of responses and postures that readers enact during the actual process of reading. By first listening to what readers have to say, instead of having them remain silent in deference to someone else's expertise, a teacher acknowledges the central role of the individual in our democratic form of social relationships. Individual responses, however, always exist within some cultural and social context.

No one has better articulated this delicate balance between the individual and the group than Louise Rosenblatt.[1] For the most part, however, her ideas have not been used to question the attitudes and social relations fostered by the conditions under which literature is normally taught. The professional community's refusal to take seriously what Rosenblatt has, in various ways, been saying since the 1920s suggests that the difficulty is not with her literary credentials or her critical aesthetic theory. Instead, what's at issue is the threat her work poses for traditional, undemocratic teaching and learning arrangements. Her guiding question has always been a subversive one: "To what extent is literary study in the schools contributing to the persistent hold of habits of thought and images of behavior no longer appropriate to our present-day knowledge and our aspirations for a more democratic way of life?"

(Rosenblatt, 1940, p. 106). Acting on her challenge would mean progressing our pedagogy from monologue to dialogue and finally entertaining the values of democracy.

Like other teachers, I believed I was honoring the responses of my students, because I was allowing them to speak their minds in open discussion. What I needed to discover was that my interest in individual acts of reading was too limited a focus. In *Literature as Exploration,* published in 1938, Rosenblatt offered a deliberate so- cial agenda for teaching and learning literature in the schools. Her comprehensive synthesis moved beyond the potential solipsism of individual response without reinvoking the dominating authority of the teacher's voice. Committed to democracy and its procedures for honoring the individual, Rosenblatt's book represented her "decla- ration that there are no generic readers or generic interpretations, but only innumerable relationships between readers and texts" (Rosenblatt, 1990, p. 104). But to encourage democratic thinking, a focus on reader response was only half the picture; the ensuing dis- cussion method was the central force of the book—and the aspect most readily ignored by its readers.

In the preface to the first edition, Rosenblatt explicitly stated the intentions behind her work: "to demonstrate that the study of literature can have a very real, and even central, relation to the points of growth in the social and cultural life of a democracy" (Rosenblatt, 1938, p. v). Having tactically deployed the word *de- mocracy,* she continued:

> Viewing literature in its relations to the diverse needs of human beings, this book will seek to answer the questions: "How can the experience and study of literature foster a sounder understanding of life and nourish the development of balanced, humane person- alities?" "How can the teacher minister to the love of literature, initiate his students into its delights, and at the same time further these broader aims?" (p. v)

With these questions in mind, an educational proposal would only be appropriate if it included some kind of transactional process that begins with the individual student and then has that student partic- ipate in sharing and contesting with other students as part of a dia- logue of inquiry and interpretation. Values are indeed the province of literature, but how they are finally understood depends very much on the *way* they are evoked and considered.

Rosenblatt's privileging of the individual reader, both inside and outside of the classroom, is always related to a dynamic *social* context that embodies the values of democracy. In *Literature as*

Exploration, Rosenblatt carries forward Dewey's central insight about the role of the receiver in constituting the art object:

> The *product* of art—temple, painting, statue, poem—is not the *work* of art. The work takes place when a human being cooperates with the product so that the outcome is an experience that is enjoyed because of its liberating and orderly properties. (Dewey, 1934/1980, p. 214)

Following Dewey's lead, she explores how this experience serves as the initiating force in the literature classroom and thus helps students assimilate "habits of thought conducive to social understanding" (Rosenblatt, 1968, p. 22). In a transactional literature classroom, where the teacher is never the sole and dominating reader, students who are "moved by a work of literature, will be led to ponder on questions of right or wrong, of admirable or antisocial qualities, of justifiable or unjustifiable actions" (1968, p. 17). The literary work, in other words, concretely embodies and dramatizes the abstractions of the social sciences and thus provides a direct means for students to consider human motives and actions.

Rosenblatt fears for the fragility of democratic social arrangements, which our selfish human temperament always seems on the verge of disrupting or tearing apart. Further, if the urge to let someone else make the decisions is not resisted early and often in our educational institutions, students will inevitably fall prey to externally imposed "solutions":

> Obviously, a rigid set of dogmatic ideas and fixed responses to specific conditions is the worst kind of equipment for the contemporary youth. As soon as actual conditions prove that his passively acquired code is useless or even harmful, he has nothing else to cling to. Having been made dependent upon ready-made props, he will be precipitated into painful insecurity. This kind of insecurity, this craving for some easy, reassuring formula, makes the youth of other countries and sometimes our own a ready prey to those enemies of democracy who hold out the delusive bait of ready-made solutions to all problems. Unprepared to think independently, the young man and woman seek to return to the infantile state in which there is no responsibility to make decisions; they are thus willing to blindly follow some "leader" whose tools and prey they become. (1968, p. 129)

The best educational defense against the *true believer,* against the mechanically automated student, is a transactional program of teaching/learning, one that reinforces each individual's faith in his or her own judgments, even as these judgments remain open to question. In this way belief is prevented from degenerating into dogma.

A tension between voluntarism and social determinism deeply animates the American experience. Looking in one direction, Americans believe that "any behavior can be interpreted as having been willed by the actor . . . the individual is free to accept or reject various modes of behavior" (1968, p. 144). In contrast to this view, many resolve themselves to the idea that "the individual is merely a kind of automaton entirely at the mercy of external pressures" (1968, p. 155). The course of human behavior might be plotted between the perils of these two shores, as on one occasion, personal interest is cultivated and the group ignored, while on the next, social constraints and blind allegiance predominate. The danger, Rosenblatt points out, lies in our democratic arrangements being unable to mediate those persons and groups who prefer a single perspective:

> The individualistic emphasis of our society builds up a frequent reluctance to see the implications for others of our own actions or to understand the validity of the needs that motivate other people's actions. The fact that the success of the individual must so often be at the expense of others places a premium on this kind of blindness. Teachers of literature need to take this cultural pressure into account, since it is so directly opposed to the attitude of mind they are attempting to foster. For literature by its very nature invokes participation in the experiences of others and comprehension of their goals and aspirations. (1968, pp. 92–93)

Ideally, Rosenblatt emphasizes, citizens in a democracy need the convictions and enthusiasms of their own responses, yet they must also keep an open mind about alternate points of view, and negotiate meanings and actions so as to respect both individual diversity and community needs (1968, pp. 184–85, 193, 223).

As we know, autocracy in one form or another has dominated recorded history. This left most individuals serving some master. Democracy broke many of these ancient ties, but not without setting new burdens. Chief among these is the feeling of alienation from the group. Such alienation is often compensated for by other-directed behavior, a phenomenon early described by de Tocqueville. To overcome this tendency to follow authority blindly, individuals require confidence in their own ability to interpret and judge what they observe around them in the world. But confident and outspoken individuals must be complemented by a tradition of conduct that reconciles differences among their responses. Such is the heart of Rosenblatt's formulation of literature education: a dialogic, back-and-forth movement between reader and text, and then a reaching outward to an ongoing social conversation with other readers and other texts.

Rosenblatt's transactional approach to the teaching of literature, with its emphasis on interpersonal classroom dialogue, also has important implications for text selection. Writing in 1940, two years after the publication of *Literature as Exploration,* Rosenblatt argued for a balance between contemporary works and the classics. Wishing to avoid "the feeling that literature is something remote, academic, something to be approached with all the decorum of the classroom," she asserts that judgment only grows through use—in a democracy it "cannot be legislated [or] imparted from above" (1940, p. 103). Individuals must continually experience for themselves and be responsible for their own reflections.

> The development of the power to discriminate, to accept what is good and to reject what is valueless in literature and in life, is frustrated by any view which sets up a body of works as "timeless classics," hence passively to be accepted as *ipse fucto* valuable, without the necessary struggle to perceive values in terms of life and literature as the student himself experiences them. (1940, p. 103)

In the transactional classroom, contemporary works figure centrally. Not only do they confront students with artistic representations of the basic problems of living, they also encourage independence in matters of valuation, since the worth of these works remains open to disagreement.

In the classroom, openly encouraging reading behavior as a lively interaction prefigures specific social values—namely, how American citizens *ought* to act if they are to reach social decisions democratically. But this relationship between school reading and social values is generally ignored. Academics narrowly concerned with literature, with the personal psychological dynamics of response (see Holland, 1975) or isolated aesthetic issues, avoid the *social* project for the reading of literature that Rosenblatt launched. Instead, many continue with "objective" research, trying to determine precisely the features and parameters of their models of reading. In doing so they provoke endless quarrels over what is the "real" transactional model. Further, when reader-response critics attempt to present full-blown descriptions of their own processes of reading or of someone else's, they often forget the social dimension of the transactional model and how it might positively influence teaching practice.

Research into how literary reading occurs can never discover a single process of response and interpretation, and any argument about whether the transactional model is sufficiently accurate in descriptive terms misses this point. Instead, her transactional model settles the conflict over how much *meaning* resides in the reader and how much is text-governed by revealing such arguments to be futile in the first place. Neither category, *text* or *reader*, exists in isolation of the other. As Rosenblatt has articulated throughout her career:

> Every transaction is unique even when the same reader and same text are involved. Of course, we can compare readings by the same or different readers with a text, but that doesn't relate to the reader-text question. In H_2O, do we ask whether the hydrogen or the oxygen is more important? We can think of reader and text as separate activities before or after the transaction—but the work (the water) exists *in* the transaction. Recall that the text is simply marks on the page. (personal correspondence, 11 July 1988)

Continuing to raise this false subject-object dichotomy, which can lead to such outlandish, relativistic claims as the words on the page offer no constraints to interpretation, is only possible when the social context is ignored.

Reader and text come together in the process of reading. Allowing any term to exist in isolation of the process that gave birth to it readily leads us to lose sight of the convening event. Donald Winnicott, for instance, once disrupted a conversation by declaring, "There's no such thing as a baby."[2] In doing this he was simply pointing out that the status of *baby* demands a *mother* and *mothering* and thus using any of these terms alone encourages a false concept of separate entities. For Rosenblatt, the poem exists as a bound reader-text composite during the reading transaction, never as separate, individual elements.

Meaning itself, as any number of contemporary critics have concluded, remains an outlaw, even as more and more elaborate apparatuses have been spun to catch and devour it. Meaning as constructive *play*, not end product, points directly to Rosenblatt's agenda. She would encourage readers to keep testing their readings with others in public and then modify them accordingly. Through this dialectic of interpretive maneuvers, the individual becomes part of a democratic, collaborative effort. What matters are the kinds of character and behavior this noncompetitive game engenders. Any actual spoils of victory, such as a finally determined and indisputable *meaning*, are irrelevant. For, as Rosenblatt demonstrates, moderation must be part of the education of the young, part of their coming to terms with the collaborative role of the text. Thus, in teaching literature, what strategies will we find to yoke the self with the group? How might we begin with the evocations of individual readers and end with the dynamics of public sharing and validation? How will we mediate alternating cycles of disagreement and consensus as our students read socially in our classrooms?

Notes

1. See Pradl, 1991, for a fuller explication of the democratic context of Rosenblatt's work.

2. Cited by Oliver Sacks. 24 May 1987. *New York Times Book Review,* p. 21.

Chapter Ten

The Impasse of Reader Response

Literary texts are central to democratic education. They affirm and confirm—through the personal acts of aesthetic evocation that are necessary to access them—the uniqueness of the *individual,* even while insisting that such acts inevitably relate to sharing and participating in the actions of a larger community. Literature embodies an ethical way of knowing, and so one reader's reading can never be adequately substituted for another's. In Rosenblatt's transactional scheme, solitary readers responding are simply never to be found. She sees group effort as supportive of individual human agency. Indeed, such effort characterizes reading in nonhierarchical, democratic classrooms in which students are continually part of the circle of praxis, moving from understanding to decision to action.

Marginalizing Rosenblatt's Agenda

The rise of reader-response criticism could have provided fertile ground for Rosenblatt's thinking to begin transforming life in the literature classroom. Yet Rosenblatt's social agenda for the reading of literature remains incompatible with traditional academic literary concerns, because she refuses to separate acts of interpretation from their pedagogical implications and consequences. Indeed, the focus of reader-response criticism has, for the most part, only been an excuse for a new formalism, as Jane Tompkins provocatively argues, not a campaign for emphasizing how words are marshaled by authors to bring about specific social effects on readers:

> Instead of moving the audience and bringing pressure to bear on the world, the work is thought to present another separate and more perfect world, which the flawed reader must labor to appropriate. The work is not a gesture in a social situation, or an ideal model for human behavior, but an interplay of formal and thematic properties to be penetrated by the critic's mind. The imputation that a poem might break out of its self-containment and perform a service would disqualify it immediately from consideration as a work of art. (Tompkins, p. 210)

When the reading and teaching of literature are disconnected from any vital relationship with how the forms of social life in a democracy are to be determined, "the art product loses its power to influence public opinion on matters of national importance" (p. 213).

In tracing the history of literature's declining influence, from the ancients to the present time, Tompkins locates a pattern whereby the individual is cultivated in splendid detachment, rather than in constant dialogue with others. For instance, the literature of feeling— sentimental and Gothic novels or the poetry of sensibility—can be viewed as having been "designed to give the reader certain kinds of emotional experience rather than to mold character or guide behavior, and is aimed at the psychic life of individuals rather than at collective standards of judgment on public issues" (p. 215). By shifting the reader's attention from a course of action to *meaning* divination, most modern literary theorizing has created a safe zone away from any practical concerns regarding life in a democracy.

Not surprisingly, Tompkins herself, despite her radical position, remains tied to a literary critical tradition that finds it convenient to ignore Rosenblatt's message. Rather than represent her with an essay in the collection *Reader-Response Criticism,* Tompkins simply provides an afterthought footnote in the introduction:

> Louise Rosenblatt deserves to be recognized as the first among the present generation of critics in this country to describe empirically the way the reader's reactions to a poem are responsible for any subsequent interpretation of it. Her work . . . raise[s] issues central to the debates that have arisen since. (p. xxvi)

Then, in her essay that concludes the collection, Tompkins uncritically lumps Rosenblatt with Fish and Holland when she remarks, "although reader-oriented critics speak of the 'poem as event' and of 'literature as experience,' meaning is still for them the object of the critical act" (p. 206). This reference to Rosenblatt's 1964 article,

"The Poem as Event," fails to provide the social context that would clearly separate her from these other critics. Rosenblatt is the one who sees important pedagogical consequences for a democracy when students are not encouraged to join collaboratively with the teacher in the evocation and interpretation of the poem, and so are frequently left with no bridge to the social consequences of particular readings.

Perhaps in literary criticism circles men are not yet sophisticated enough to be pointed in a completely new direction by a woman. Still, in the rush to take credit for the discovery of the reader, the systematic neglect of Rosenblatt's work is striking. In *Reception Theory*, for example, Robert Holub separates reader-response theory from reception theory, which, of course, allows him to ignore Rosenblatt completely. Holub does, however, offer a possible reason for Wolfgang Iser's neglect of her ideas—the German intellectual context out of which Iser works is not eclectic, but functions as an independent and tightly knit group. Yet if this is true, why does Iser, in *The Act of Reading*, draw on Dewey's *Art and Experience* and also refer to Norman Holland? Similarly, William Ray, as part of a thorough treatment of reader response in his book, *Literary Meaning*, includes extensive chapters on Iser, Holland, Bleich, and Fish, but mentions Rosenblatt not once.

Steven Mailloux, more kindly disposed to Rosenblatt, refers to her twice in his book *Interpretive Conventions*, which otherwise concentrates on "five influential theories of the literary reading process: those of Stanley Fish, Norman Holland, David Bleich, Wolfgang Iser, and Jonathan Culler" (Mailloux, 1982, p. 9). His hesitancy to devote more space to Rosenblatt becomes especially ironic when he claims that he favors those critics more devoted to a "social model of reading" (i.e., Fish, Iser, and Culler) as opposed to those who invoke "psychological categories such as individual selves and unique identities" (p. 9). Mailloux does acknowledge that "Rosenblatt argued for the pedagogical relevance of the reader's individual experience of literature," and he mentions Rosenblatt's attempt to separate herself from the "aggressively subjective approaches" of Bleich and Holland (p. 37). But, in the same breath, he notes that her work derives from William James. This supposedly connects her to Iser, who was influenced by the phenomenology of Edmund Husserl, also someone indebted to James (p. 37). One then has to wonder why—after Mailloux writes, "During the hegemony of intrinsic criticism, only a few literary theorists like Louise Rosenblatt and Kenneth Burke ventured outside the text to discuss the reader" (pp. 66–67)—he neglects to follow this lead.

Indeed, Mailloux's next sentence reads, "Later, Wayne Booth helped begin the project of reestablishing talk about readers through his influential *Rhetoric of Fiction,* which contained discussions of the novel's effects on its audience" (p. 67).[1] This version of literary history only serves to keep yet another woman critic at the margins—Vernon Lee. In *The Handling of Words and Other Studies in Literary Psychology,* which includes essays written as long ago as the 1890s, Lee focused on how rhetorical structures in literature affect readers in particular ways: "Each Reader, while receiving from the Writer, is in reality reabsorbing into his life, where it refreshes or poisons him, a residue of his own living; but melted into absorbable subtleness, combined and stirred into a new kind of efficacy by the choice of the Writer" (Lee, p. 79). However fascinating Lee's work may have been, it was obviously not *influential,* since reputations depend very much on the networks that endorse and promote them.

In a subsequent essay, however, Mailloux partially redeems himself by explicitly considering why Rosenblatt has been "strangely overlooked." He speculates that her "work and its implicit neo-pragmatism had to be 'forgotten' in order for the new reader-response criticism to establish its theoretical ethos and carry out a decade of intense theoretical debate over the question of its 'epistemological skepticism'" (Mailloux, 1990, p. 40). This interpretation acknowledges Rosenblatt's dismantling of the reader/text distinction, in accordance with the transactional vocabulary put forward by Dewey and Bentley in *Knowing and the Known.* This dismantling had already solved the problems that the later reader-response critics used in part to build their careers in academia. Accordingly, to bring Rosenblatt into their conversation as an equal would have rendered many of their proposals obsolete.

Continuing his discussion of pragmatism's refusal to take foundationalism seriously, Mailloux points out how pragmatism "denies the subject-object split and rejects the notion that there needs to be a theory of knowledge that regulates the relationship between a knower and an object known" (p. 41). Thus, having allied her reading theory with this "pragmatist rejection of traditional epistemology," Rosenblatt actually changed the nature of the debate by "figuring the poem as a transactive event" (p. 41). In advance, she had set aside "the very question that fueled [a] decade of reader-response critical theory: is it the reader or the text that determines interpretation?" (p. 41).

After these promising revelations, however, Mailloux chooses not to continue his reading of Rosenblatt's ideas, but instead devotes the remainder of his essay to the five reader-response critics he had previously covered in *Interpretive Conventions*. Also, significantly, nowhere else in the volume where Mailloux's essay appears is there any reference to Rosenblatt. Yet what was being reported included conversations at two Summer Institutes for Teachers of Literature to Undergraduates (Myrtle Beach SC, 1987 and 1988) that "focused on current topics in the teaching of literature: post-structuralism, cultural criticism, reader-response theory, and issues of gender and the canon" (Moran and Penfield, p. 1). Only Janet Emig expressed any outrage that radical critical theory mostly leaves classroom practices completely untouched (Moran and Penfield, pp. 87–96).

Despite Mailloux's insights, reader-response criticism remains a school of textual analysis rather than an encompassing literary stance with implications for all types of readings. This is perhaps most starkly illustrated by how reader response is represented in a recent student edition of James Joyce's *A Portrait of the Artist as a Young Man*. It is merely one of "five contemporary critical perspectives" providing an introduction to "the current critical and theoretical ferment in literary studies" (Murfin, p. iii), the others being psychoanalytic, feminist, deconstructionist, and new historicist. While he does refer to Rosenblatt, the author of this account totally misses the point of her transactional message when he hauls out the epistemological questions she'd already settled:

> Just who *is* the reader? (or, to place the emphasis differently, Just who is *the* reader?) Aren't you reader-response critics just talking about your own idiosyncratic responses when you describe what a line from *Paradise Lost* "does" in and to "the reader's" mind? What about my responses? What if they're different? Will you be willing to say that all responses are equally valid? (Murfin, p. 273)

Presenting reader response in this manner, as merely another theoretical problem to be solved, shrewdly exempts teacher-centered pedagogy from having to change.

Anticipating the Cultural Critics

Improperly identifying Rosenblatt with reader-response criticism allows her to be neglected by the cultural critics, whose approach she both anticipated and transcended. With the sociopolitical emphasis that has emerged in the current poststructuralist phase of criticism, it is popular (especially among Marxists) to use the techniques of reading to disclose underlying assumptions, the network of ideological constraints that determine both a reader's reading and being. Having discovered the reader, teachers of this persuasion now meticulously seek to demonstrate to their students how they as readers are socially constructed and are therefore often deceived by textual ideology, whether by gender, race, or class.

This armory of defensive or resistant reading strategies has grown swiftly (see Mellor et al, 1991, and Moon, 1990). Rightly, these educators encourage teachers to be politically aware in order to challenge conventional beliefs and the marginalization of the powerless. By insisting, once and for all, that reading is neither neutral nor innocent, they raise new and challenging questions such as, How might impressionable young women be supervised in their reading of juvenile romances, which seek to shape stereotypic domestic longings? (see Christian-Smith, 1990). Their own teaching maneuvers, however, are seldom innocent or neutral; often, the main interest is attacking Western ideology.

Initially, we might be inclined to include Rosenblatt with this group of critics, given her background in anthropology and her frequent consideration of the social, moral, and psychological assumptions that inform the literary work as experienced by students. But there is a crucial difference: Rosenblatt has never believed that the individual is created, *written,* solely by the culture, by its codes and conventions. Further, although the cultural critics are supposedly concerned with altering human relationships in the classroom, there is the danger that their theoretical analyses merely serve as content for the next "liberating" lecture. When teachers only employ theory this way, it contributes to alienating the general public from literature. As Rosenblatt has noted, "If anyone is to blame for the declining interest in literature, it's the academicians and critics who have given us theories of the literary work that neglect the transaction between text and reader" (Rosenblatt, 1981, p. 13).

Unlike those critics who use *disclosure* to paint a negative picture of Western values, values they see as subjugating the individual to subservience under capitalism, Rosenblatt insists on helping students *discriminate* between what should be rejected and what should be retained and strengthened. This kind of critical discrimination requires the values of democracy:

> Any system of values can be scrutinized in terms of its consequences for human life. Any form of conduct, any social mechanism, any custom or institution, should be measured in terms of its actual effect on the individual personalities that make up the society. . . . This rests upon belief in the fundamental dignity and worth of the human being. It sets up the well-being and fulfillment of the individual in opposition to any abstractions for which might be claimed a superior reality or value such as the Elect, the Super-

man, the Proletariat, the Nation, the Race, or the State. This basic
postulate of value is obviously one that receives support from
many elements present in our cultural heritage. (Rosenblatt, 1968,
pp. 165–66)

While the cultural critics justify their own covert indoctrination of
anti-democratic attitudes by insisting that all teaching ultimately in-
doctrinates political attitudes, Rosenblatt answers them when she
challenges all teachers to indoctrinate openly the basic concepts of a
democratic system. Working explicitly on the basis of democratic
principles helps to defend students from being subtly indoctrinated
with negative attitudes toward our society. It preserves students' freedom to make up their own minds about what to accept and what to
reject. Further, it sees literature study as part of a broader movement
to foster constructive social transformation, while avoiding the alienation unwittingly invited by the cultural critics.

Misreading Rosenblatt in Practice

Despite a hesitancy in literature education to talk about democratic
values and relationships, citations to Rosenblatt's work now regu-
larly dot the landscape of writings on English teaching. But discovering the reader seldom represents a democratic strategy for
reconsidering authority in the classroom. Instead, many teachers
who do cite Rosenblatt isolate what she says about the reader by
largely ignoring her social implications.[2]

Anne Ruggles Gere and her colleagues at the University of
Michigan, in compiling an otherwise imaginative text for working
with future English teachers, provide one example of how the social
force of Rosenblatt's theory has been muted. Accurately, they indicate that reading responses evolve and change:

> Even as she insists on the unique nature of individual experiences
> with literature, however, Rosenblatt emphasizes that these trans-
> actions can be complete only if the initial response is open to
> modification by further acquaintance with the text. Students
> should continue to look closely at the text and let their views
> change and grow in response to it. (Gere et al, p. 153)

But, because Gere and her colleagues lock themselves into a four-
part taxonomy—language as either artifact, development, expression, or social construct—for cataloging approaches to teaching
English, they are forced to lump Rosenblatt with the reader-
response critics:

> The theories of Rosenblatt, Bleich, and Holland all emphasize a point important to the language-as-expression classroom: Students' responses to literary texts differ, and those differences should be valued. Reading is an individual act, not a generic one, and the teacher's role is not to provide the "correct" response but to welcome the multiple readings engendered by a given text and then help students move toward richer understandings. (p. 153)

This allows them to ignore completely Rosenblatt's democratic concerns. Gere does acknowledge the limitations of each approach and urges teachers to continue to criticize and improve all methods. No democratic criteria, however, are offered for judging the social arrangements emphasized by any given approach.

"Student-centered," "celebrates individuality," "promotes independence and creativity," and "values feelings" are listed as the "potentials" of the "Language as Expression" approach. Its "limitations" include "privileges feeling over thinking," "is more individualistic than social," "privileges student texts and responses over professional texts and responses," and "is loosely structured" (pp. 158–61). By isolating Rosenblatt in this category, Gere encourages the mistaken notion that the transactional project exists free of any social agenda. This also prevents Rosenblatt's ideas from influencing Gere's Language as Social Construct approach, which, among other things, "promotes high expectations" and "teaches critical, political, and social skills" (pp. 194–95). Once again, when Rosenblatt's ideas are segregated, one is left with an incomplete understanding of the role played by readers' responses in a democratic literature classroom.

For those literature teachers who do pay closer attention to the broader scope of Rosenblatt's transactional theory, collaboration assumes an important focus. This theme, for example, is reflected in several of the teaching goals that one teacher outlined in trying to understand for himself the pattern of Rosenblatt's ideas:

- Our teaching of literature should be about relations between texts and readers rather than relations between extracted meaning and readers.
- Talk in the classroom should not be dominated by the teacher. Students should listen to each other.
- Most important, we should support each other in reading rather than compete with each other. (Martin, pp. 57–59)

Although there is no explicit claim here for a democratic social agenda, the classroom space is seen as providing occasions for students to support one another as they test ideas and learn from each other. The teacher joins this democratic conversation instead of dictatorially dominating it. Honoring reader response in this instance establishes the learning base for productive social participation.

Other instances of the power of collaboration are reported in a special issue of *English Leadership Quarterly* devoted to "The Changing Literature Classroom." Prompted by Rosenblatt's ideas, two teachers at Mesa State College in Colorado devised a plan that engaged freshman honors students in a group writing project on the poems of Robert Frost. After drawing out individual student readings, these teachers concentrated on sharing, discussing, and mediating disparate viewpoints and conclusions. This disruption in the regular, expected routine often filled the class with frustration. In the end, however, student testimony validated the learning purposes behind Rosenblatt's transactional project:

> What we did do was to learn and evaluate, good and bad, the tricky process of how to work together and how to discover Frost in our own eyes. We were allowed to be original thinkers. We were allowed to experience and expand our knowledge of a poet personally without being told our views were wrong or outside of accepted literary convention. *That* is what is a big deal. (Broughton and Rider, p. 9)

Response was not an end in itself, but was meant to encourage movement between self and group. Without social exchange, there is no way to arrive at critical reflection, the basis for altering one's original responses and conceptions—again a democratic protocol without naming it as such.

Despite such positive examples, including the work of others such as Robert Probst (1988) and Patrick Dias (1987), we still must wonder why Rosenblatt's thinking has become so misshapen in the hands of many well-meaning teachers. In the politics of academia, of course, it's difficult to dislodge vested interests of any sort. Certainly, a narrow reader-response gloss of her transactional theory allowed it to be slotted conveniently into traditional critical approaches and thus pedagogy could be satisfied with the mere appearance of change. Another reason for our resisting Rosenblatt's central message, however, might stem from how unsettling we find her ideas about constructive thinking.

Integrating Reason and Feeling

In the original, 1938 edition of *Literature as Exploration,* Rosenblatt emphasizes the intimate connection between how we handle experiences in actual life and how our mind joins with the literary text in feeling through it and in making sense of it: "There is more than a verbal parallel between the process of reflective thinking based on response to literature and the process of reflection as a prelude to action in life itself" (1938, p. 267). Next, she refers to Dewey, who "reminded us that in actual life constructive thinking usually starts as a result of some conflict or discomfort, or when habitual behavior is impeded and a choice of new paths of behavior must be made" (1938, p. 267). By understanding the role of conflict in constructive thinking, and all of the uncertainty it entails, I suddenly recognize how resistant I can be to incorporating it into my teaching.

Most of my intellectual energy is directed at resolving or removing conflict. Thus, understandably, I think of conflict initially as something negative, as something to be avoided. Thinking, however, is precisely what "grows out of some sort of tension, some emotional impulse, and is colored by it" (1938, p. 267). In this sense, my emotions and ideas are always intertwined when I direct my full resources at those things that I cannot predict or control in advance. Problem solving is a natural human endeavor, and it's triggered by tension, which serves as "the impetus toward seeking some solution, but intelligent behavior is the result of thought brought to bear upon the problem" (p. 267). In other words, "the validity of the thought will usually depend on the extent to which emotion has been controlled or has been prevented from obscuring the actual situation before us" (p. 268).

The most significant tension in a person's life is bound to be social in origin. Therefore, the question is always: What will we do when faced with new relationships in new situations? As Rosenblatt argues, my "first need is to understand [my] own emotional response to the person or situation" (1938, p. 266). This means realizing "to what extent [I am] dominated by preoccupations and prejudices that may have led [me] to exaggerate some things, ignore others, and thus not to have fully understood them" (p. 266). Further, I must bring my "basic moral or psychological assumptions out into the open in order to test the validity of their application to this new situation"(p. 266).

Under such scrutiny, I may discover that my "own past experience and information must be supplemented before [I] can make an adequate judgment or plan appropriate action" (p. 266). And, indeed, my original reactions may require revision or even rejection. As Dewey noted:

> . . . in the arts proper, we can not only modify our own attitude so
> as to effect useful preparation for what is to happen, but we can
> modify the happening itself. This use of one change or perceptible

occurrence as a sign of others and as a means of preparing ourselves, did not wait for the development of modern science. It is as old as man himself, being the heart of all intelligence. (Dewey, 1960, p. 132)

This ongoing process of reaction, reflection, and revision marks a mature person's innovative and productive encounters in life.

The flux of contingent human events, however, is such that in education, when we attempt to study these same events, we tend to segregate theory from practice. Yet our attempts at separating life in the classroom from the bustle of everyday living often creates thought situations that are free of feeling and emotion:

> It is comparatively easy for the students to think rationally about difficult human problems when impersonal academic treatments make them abstract subjects of thought. Unfortunately, that kind of thinking is probably not very useful; it lacks the conflicting impulses or emotional perplexities out of which thinking usually grows in real life. (Rosenblatt, 1938, p. 268)

Reason only flows as the issue of feeling. This is a key insight I keep avoiding. Whenever I settle into a nonreflective routine, I don't have to expend the emotional energy required to keep response open and changing. It seems safer locked inside the abstractions of my mind than to engage in the mess of feelings.

Rosenblatt further emphasizes this juncture between reason and feeling by quoting a passage from Dewey's *Human Nature and Conduct:*

> The conclusion is not that the emotional, passionate phase of action can be or should be eliminated in behalf of a bloodless reason. More "passions," not fewer, is the answer. To check the influence of hate there must be sympathy, while to rationalize sympathy there are needed emotions of curiosity, caution, respect for the freedom of others—dispositions, which evoke objects which balance those called up by sympathy, and prevent its degeneration into maudlin sentiment and meddling interference. Rationality, once more, is not a force to evoke against impulse and habit. It is the attainment of a working harmony among diverse desires. (Dewey, 1922, pp. 170–71)

This is the fundamental lesson for educational decisions carried out in a democracy. For, after quoting Dewey, Rosenblatt offers her most resounding challenge: "We teachers should recognize much more clearly than we do the possibilities in literary materials for furthering that kind of rationality" (1938, p. 269). In the process of transacting with a text, emotion and reason form an essential partnership:

> [Literature] may provide the emotional tension and conflicting at-
> titudes out of which may spring the kind of thinking that can later
> be assimilated into actual behavior. The emotional character of the
> student's response to literature offers an opportunity for helping
> him to develop the ability *to think rationally within the context of*
> *an emotionally colored situation.* Furthermore, the teaching situ-
> ation . . . in which a group of students and a teacher exchange
> views and stimulate one another toward clearer understanding can
> contribute greatly toward the development of such habits of reflec-
> tion. (p. 269)

This conception of *constructive thinking* encourages us to face the
fury and unpredictability of emotion, which by the nature of things
will always initially appear out of control and therefore uncontrol-
lable—living life in the uncertainty lane. But that's the promise of
democracy. Vulnerability. Trust. Improvisation. Everything seems
turned on its head when as teacher I'm preparing myself to listen,
not to act as if I know in advance.

Teachers of English, Rosenblatt is forever reminding us, contribute in important ways to creating the character of future citizens.
When we engage openly and reflectively with the conflicting emotions and interpretations that literature evokes, we are living the
very essence of democracy. For "if we only do justice to potentiali-
ties inherent in literature itself," as Rosenblatt declared, "we can
make a vital social contribution" (1968, p. 274).

> As the student vicariously shares through literature the emotions
> and aspirations of other human beings, he can gain heightened
> sensitivity to the needs and problems of others remote from him in
> temperament, in space, or in social environment; he can develop
> a greater imaginative capacity to grasp the meaning of abstract
> laws or political and social theories for actual human lives. Such
> sensitivity and imagination are part of the indispensable equip-
> ment of the citizen of a democracy. (p. 274)

By not limiting transactionalism to reader response, we come to
understand that Rosenblatt's seminal contribution derives from her
social concerns for democracy as they are translated into an agenda
for individual readers. How then might we extend student evocations of the poem and thus promote reasoned discourse as the basis
for decision making and action taking? How will we strike a creative balance between self and group to expand each student's freedom and possibilities?

Notes

1. Interestingly, in the foreword to the most recent edition of *Literature as Exploration* (1995), Wayne Booth himself finally joins the chorus of those now acknowledging Rosenblatt's achievement: "I doubt that any other literary critic of this century has enjoyed and suffered as sharp a contrast of powerful influence and absurd neglect as Louise Rosenblatt."

2. It is important to note, however, that even just acknowledging the reader's active participation in the act of reading represents a significant advance over previous teacher- and text-centered pedagogies. Indeed, this may be sowing seeds for a future when teachers and students might, together, entertain broader social concerns.

Chapter Eleven

Entering the Dance of Conversation

Truly productive moments in the classroom center around disagreements. Dissent, not assent, stimulates our minds. Disagreement provokes us to imagine perspectives not yet within our horizon. Yet once a traditional "lesson" is securely on track, the spontaneity of listening quickly vanishes and any genuine disagreements a student might express are dismissed as breaches of social etiquette. The teacher would like all responses predicted in advance—maybe that's why classrooms are often such joyless places. Still, if disagreement is to be a key ingredient of classroom talk, we will be obliged to mediate its disruptive force.

Disagreement is not necessarily adversarial and thus threatening to the social fabric. Ideally, we disagree in order to test and revise our thinking, not to be disagreeable. Constructive disagreement occurs when we feel comfort and trust together. In conversation, an important goal is to keep repairing disagreements even while provoking new ones.

When productive talk occurs, we need not ask who's in control of the classroom. Once we're prepared to give up our fixed script as teacher, we begin to engage in democratic processes with students— sharing an improvisational dance, expressing "what if" propositions, no longer burdened with an endless supply of premeditated answers. Often, we end our conversational contributions with some question or simply pass the baton with an invitation: "And what are your thoughts on this matter?" Valuing controversy allows us to discover that conversation is, fundamentally, an ethical act of communion.

Without disagreement, the ties of relationship remain largely invisible. For when it is nonadversarial, noncompetitive, disagreement always works toward agreement. Disagreement serves to highlight the enterprise held in common, while the agreement we reach, in this sense, entails understanding, not coercion because it anticipates more questioning. The to and fro of conversation keeps our views open to scrutiny when we're committed to the matter at hand. In this sense, we play with distinctions and so move beyond our differences.

Persons establish good faith in dialogue by mutually consenting to be vulnerable on the condition that such openness will not be exploited. Until we feel safe, we are hesitant to begin any dialogue in which we may be revealing our imperfections. But how do we come to feel safe? There are at least two options. If we understand *safe* to be a condition that we're solely responsible for controlling, then to feel safe is to cover up our errors or faults in advance, so no one else can see them and expose us to the pain of ridicule. In such a state, we perform, we don't dialogue. On the other hand, *safe* can refer to a condition that we help to create with others, in which there are no hurtful consequences when we show ourselves to be less than perfect.

Still, we have to face up to the fact that revealing limitations, in order to remain open to learning and thus open to change, is a risky and tiring business. It is not easy to trust each other. Accordingly, talk in the classroom often rejects what is happening at the margins, because it doesn't fit with the particular operating script that the teacher is using. How do we wait for connections not yet voiced or even imagined without giving in to an anxiety for closure? How do we ensure that everyone's perspective exists on an equal footing?

Searching for Conversational Models

Deplorably, most public debate, like that heard coming from the halls of Congress, involves adversarial posturing, a litany of previously scripted and disputatious sermonettes or lectures—and this has helped give the art of disagreement a bad name. Members harangue each other rather than openly *debate.* Arguments are not scrutinized for flaws nor is there any direct response to criticism. Of course, for debate to happen, speakers must agree to be open to evidence and reason, but this implies a mutual transaction, not a one-way passage. In other words, the way in which people are associating is important. As Sandra Stotsky suggests in her critique of the role of language in civic education, the way "people resolve disagreement or seek to effect change in others critically influences the nature of their political relationships to each other" (Stotsky, p. 197). Yet, regrettably, to speak in tentative imagining terms, to take on previously untried ideas and roles, poses a severe threat to a politician's image and status; no one wants to risk the media branding them forever on the basis of some exploratory utterance.

Somewhere in government, however, the conversation of genuine exploration and negotiation occurs. In closed committee sessions or in White House policy meetings, views that are not finally fixed are actually aired. Unfortunately, all the public overhears are impermeable speeches and flashy soundbites, and these hardly provide models for the discourse of exploration and compromise that citizens need if they are to succeed in their daily lives where they both work and compete together. Most of the discourse we see in the public arena is already solidified and even media interviews allow participants to repeat previously held positions rather than shape new understandings in their very acts of speaking.

When was the last time a public official admitted in open dialogue, "Gee, I hadn't thought of that before"? No wonder we are left with the impression that disputes are not healthy, do not lead to improvement and consensus. The point is always to be right—not experimental, reflective, or playfully inventive. Monologue seems to predominate in an age that otherwise is remarkable for its array of clamoring voices. And in schools, much effort is spent keeping students from talking together to seek joint solutions to assignments. As Albert Shanker, among others, has noted, "students are expected to do things by themselves. But, in the real world, people usually work and solve problems as teams or by helping each other."[1]

Struggling back to an ethics of conversation requires lowering the volume and seeing that speaker and listener belong together. Sam Ellenport drives this point home with his parody of disruptive conversational behavior: "Nine Robert's Rules for the 1990s," including,

> *Point of Personal Outrage:* At any time during a meeting when a participant becomes upset, he or she shall have the right to interrupt any other speaker without recognition from the Chair, and speak at a volume considerably higher than required for normal conversation.
>
> *Point of Personal Attack:* In response to a point raised by another speaker, the participant shall have the right to launch a personal attack without discussing the point itself.
>
> *Point of Posturing:* This entitles the participant to make reference to any literary quotation that allegedly supports his or her point of view regardless of the accuracy of the quotation.

Point of Grudge: Entitles the participant to raise an issue debated within the last 10 years for which the participant has not yet forgiven those involved.[2]

Other rules include Point of Irrelevant Interjection, Point of Contempt, Point of Harassment, Point of Redundant Information, and Point of Redundancy. Such behavior becomes all too real when our talk shows disrespect for others and doesn't serve to build consensus and community.

The Lessons of Michael Oakeshott and Gabriel Tarde

Replacing antagonistic dissonance with constructive harmony is a high priority of the political philosopher Michael Oakeshott, who sees "conversation not as a scored recitative but as a spontaneously improvised dance in which each participant responds to the movements of the other" (Auspitz, p. 354). To remember that every conversation has *already begun* before any particular set of participants has joined together is to suggest that conversations are best entered obliquely. First, check the flow and rhythm to see how the currents are moving. The contradictions of this dance involve the gentle movement toward shared leading, but this horizontal arrangement can only occur if the dance is about itself and not one partner's power.

Conversation for Oakeshott "is non-hierarchical, non-directive, and non-assertive. In a conversation, as opposed to a disputation, one voice cannot hope to dominate the others. There is no fixed agenda. There is no standard external to the conversation itself by which to judge the utterances made" (Auspitz, p. 356). This means that conversations are inherently open and unresolved as they constantly break free of the systems and constraints that would bring about a dogmatic turn and imposition. In Oakeshott's words,

> In a conversation the participants are not engaged in an inquiry or a debate; there is no "truth" to be discovered, no proposition to be proved, no conclusion sought. They are not concerned to inform, to persuade, or refute one another, and therefore the cogency of their utterances does not depend upon their all speaking the same idiom; they may differ without disagreeing. Of course, a conversation may have passages of argument and a speaker is not forbidden to be demonstrative; but reasoning is neither sovereign nor alone, and the conversation itself does not compose an argument. (Auspitz, pp. 356–57)

Because it's not meant to accomplish anything directly, conversation offers individuals an important time for invention and consolidation.

Because agreement and caring provide the basis for genuine conversation, its practice lies at the heart of democratic citizenship. Conversation not only binds us together as a people, it provides the forum in which ideas must survive criticism before they lead to some form of consensual social action. Conversation is where the endless tension between individual and group is balanced. In the words of Gabriel Tarde, a nineteenth century French sociologist:

> From the point of view of ethics, conversation battles constantly and with frequent success against egoism, against the tendency of behavior to follow entirely individual ends. . . . It tends to bring judgments of taste into agreement, eventually succeeds in doing so, and thus elaborates a poetic art, an aesthetic code which is sovereign and obeyed in each era and in each country. Conversation thus works powerfully for civilization, of which politeness and art are the primary conditions. (Tarde, pp. 313–14)

By connecting people with a set of collaborative affiliations, conversation serves the democratic principle of inclusion.

Tarde viewed conversation as central to the workings of a democracy because he understood its *purposelessness* in the best sense. Thus his definition of conversation—"any dialogue without direct and immediate utility, in which one talks primarily to talk, for pleasure, as a game, out of politeness" (p. 308)—served to emphasize the intensity of engagement that occurs among participants. It is this concentrated focus, according to Tarde, that makes conversation "the strongest agent of imitation, of the propagation of sentiments, ideas, and modes of action" (p. 309).

> Interlocutors act on each other from close at hand, not by language alone but by the tone of their voices, glances, physiognomy, magnetic gestures. It is rightly said of a good conversationalist that he is a *charmer* in the magical sense of the word. Telephone conversations, which lack the majority of these interesting elements, tend to be boring unless they are purely utilitarian. (p. 309)

The strength of open, face-to-face talk in fostering liberal sentiments is keenly recognized by despots of all sorts and, therefore,

> they keep a close and wary eye on talk between their subjects and prevent them as much as possible from conversing. Authoritarian housekeepers do not like to see their servants talk with those from elsewhere, because they know that it is in this way that they "get ideas into their heads." (p. 309)

Championing the free exchange of opinion, Tarde stressed the distinction between "obligatory conversation—regulated and ritual ceremony" and "voluntary conversation." Since "the latter generally takes place among equals" (p. 311), it is fostered by the kind of equality found in democratic organizations, which in turn contributes to reducing the regimented and artificial pageantry that helps prop up authoritarian regimes.

Not surprisingly, however, Tarde's reflections on conversation were directed at a world dominated by the privileges of men—"it is necessary for men to talk among themselves to create the prestige which must rule them" (p. 314). This gender bias is precisely the devil we continue to struggle with today as we try to reach beyond the adversarial nature of status that poisons many conversational ventures. If our goal is a conversational model that stitches mutual meaning together, even as it accommodates abrasions and separateness, then one source of inspiration is to imagine a marriage between a kind of critical talk, which has been influenced by male philosophical thinking, and a kind of caring talk, which often typifies women's discourse. But to do this, men must first rethink many of their social roles and prerogatives. Change will not occur without some realignments in the "superior" status men have perennially enjoyed.

Listening to Women

In her extraordinarily successful book *You Just Don't Understand,* Deborah Tannen reveals the entrenched male position. She outlines how women and men often hold quite opposite goals for conversation and in turn exhibit contrasting styles of speaking and listening:

> Some men really *don't* want to listen at length because they feel it frames them as subordinate. Many women do want to listen, but they expect it to be reciprocal—I listen to you now; you listen to me later. They become frustrated when they do the listening now and now and now, and later never comes. (Tannen, p. 143)

The *confusion,* as Tannen describes it in her numerous examples, may seem simple, but the status issues run deep. Because men are constantly caught up in avoiding the appearance of subordination, their talk is often competitively positioned against the talk of other participants. As Tannen notes,

> Men who approach conversations as a contest are likely to expend effort not to support the other's talk but to lead the conversation in

another direction, perhaps one in which they can take center stage
by telling a story or joke or displaying knowledge. But in doing so,
they expect their conversational partners to mount resistance. . . .
[Women] see steering the conversation in a different direction not as
a move in a game, but as a violation of the rules of the game. (p. 215)

The opposing male and female agendas are not just topical, nor are
they merely the result of jockeying for attention. More profound
psychological differences are being played out.

Carol Gilligan identifies an important disparity between the
sexes, which suggests an explanation for our differing conversational moves:

The danger men describe in their stories of intimacy is a danger of
entrapment or betrayal, being caught in a smothering relationship
or humiliated by rejection and deceit. In contrast, the danger
women portray in their tales of achievement is a danger of isolation, a fear that in standing out or being set apart by success, they
will be left alone. (Gilligan, p. 42)

While recognizing that these attributions are not meant to characterize rigidly all males or all females, it is useful to keep reflecting on
the extent to which talk and listening are governed by opposing
views of relationship: one group struggles to hold themselves apart,
another to bring themselves together. Thus, teachers who consider
knowledge to be a separate, isolated entity, and therefore value abstract talk and hierarchy as a means to order, can contribute to the
alienation many students feel in school. There is a double irony
when students hang out in the corridors in order to belong to the
community of their peers, but don't attend classes, which seem to
hold no place for them.

The way many men have been brought up makes them more
compatible with an academic environment that increasingly re-
wards purely theoretical realms of knowing and, accordingly, is
judgmental and competitive. The question is how to break this
"male" cycle, because, even in the economic sphere, it proves highly dysfunctional:

Male children are more likely to be socialized to "prevail" over other
males. That may be useful in hand-to-hand combat or in wartime. But
it is an enormously costly and destructive way to organize our
economy and carry out production. Corporate takeovers seem often
to represent an abstract battlefield. No one names these corporate
struggles correctly: street fights. (Freedman, p. 23)

The challenge is to begin acknowledging a kind of knowing that
many women have experienced before the system shut them out.

Women develop knowledge by staying connected with their feelings. This connectedness allows them to hear their own voice and to place their voice in relationship to other voices through a series of complex and intersecting narratives, rather than to separate themselves from what they are learning. But how hard it is to resist the expositions of a dominant male epistemology that favors verticality and compartmentalization. Such gender categories, of course, are not either/or, but they do reflect observable tendencies and point to the disadvantages experienced by those who resist the master discourse.

In her analysis of the linguistic power games in public institutions, Robin Lakoff examines the dilemma faced by women when they have to deny their desire for community in order to establish their separateness and thus obtain success within an elaborately defined hierarchy. How can there be a compromise between aggression and deference when men conclude that there is nothing to be gained by changing their style? "What would compensate for the loss of that sense of control that the linguistic forms of hierarchy and mastery bring with them?" (Lakoff, p. 207). Women often seem caught:

> [Their] assertive behavior is misidentified as aggression. In fact, any move away from traditional deference is seen by many men (and women) as a threat, as "pushy" or "bitchy." On the other hand, traditional female behavior is also suspect in nontraditional female circumstances. (p. 207)

Yet, even if it is not rewarded, a female sensibility has developed, one directed toward collaboration and consensus. This sensibility "has always been the cohesive force holding communities together and staving off annihilation, even as men's ways bring us ever closer to the brink"(p. 207).

So how do these differential patterns of gender-related discourse develop? Do they reflect true sex differences or are they merely the inevitable result of the larger practice of male domination in our society? Recent studies indicate that even girls and boys as young as four years old approach relational disagreements in differing ways. After looking at the conversations of 138 four- to nine-year-olds, from the middle to upper middle class, Campbell Leaper concluded that the speech acts of boys were more "controlling," while those of the girls were more "collaborative."[3] In a study of more than one thousand quarrels engaged in by twenty-four five- to seven-year-olds, who were racially and socially diverse, Patrice Miller and her colleagues found the boys to be "more concerned with and more forceful in pursuing their own agenda," while the girls were "more concerned with maintaining interpersonal harmony." In this study, it was also shown that girls tended to change their speech styles depending on whether they were talking with boys or other girls. Another researcher, Amy Sheldon, cautions against any system of speech style categories that "inadvertently values, or at least emphasizes a masculine mode of brute force over a feminine mode of conflict mitigation." Instead, Sheldon points to the girl's ability to shift speech style as a valuable "double-voice discourse." The "dual orientation" of the conflict talk of the three- and four-year-old girls allows the speaker to negotiate her "own agenda while simultaneously orienting toward the viewpoint of [her] partner." This style of talk allows for "self-assertion" to be "enmeshed in addressee-oriented mitigation."

Whether or not these divergent gender roles are socially constructed, there is much testimony about how they constrain members of both sexes. In recounting his experiences as a first-grade teacher, Daniel Meier speaks of having to assume an unnatural pose during the hiring interviews he had with principals. He couldn't just say how much he loved being with and helping young children explore the world, from Winnie the Pooh to messy poster paints on paper; instead, he had to present himself as a researcher interested in observing the intellectual growth of children's minds:

> I gave that answer to those principals, who were mostly male, because I thought they wanted a "male" response. This meant talking about intellectual matters. If I had taken a different course and talked about my interest in helping children in their emotional development, it would have been seen as closer to a "female" answer. I even altered my language, not once mentioning the word "love" to describe what I do indeed love about teaching. My answer worked; every principal nodded approvingly. (Meier, p. 56)

Such turning away from one's honest feelings may work in the short term, but in the long run it weakens each person's ability to engage in open dialogue and prevents them from finding their rightful place in the world.

Literature and Conversation

Because the reading of literature is a social act, it can serve to initiate the kinds of conversations welcomed by a democracy. But this will only be true if we ask how our conversational exchanges serve to shape, extend, and alter our responses to texts—how our social talk draws out what we feel and think about ourselves and the world. We need to resist the intrusions of status and power, otherwise the goals of equity and reciprocity will remain but a dream.

Most studies of discussion in the literature classroom reveal that students are constantly forced to decide between voicing their own responses and predicting the teacher's answers. James Marshall, among others, has found that teachers continue to judge what students have to say in terms of how it pushes everyone down a predetermined road toward the "correct" interpretation. Even in an open-ended forum, there appears to be little room for *purposelessness*. In contrast, Marshall found that the talk of students who were operating in small groups independent of the teacher was more conversational (see Marshall, 1989). Similarly, the kind of talk that occurs in adult book-discussion groups encourages improvisational building on top of previously recorded reactions, something that is only possible when listening is facilitating, rather than directing.

It can be no surprise that literature classes are often seen as a female haven and the discussion of literature a female occupation. Reading literature can be portrayed as an escape from the rough and tumble of the real world, a world dominated by the constant struggle to survive amid conditions of scarcity. Further, literature is suspect because it feeds our interest in values and the motives behind human conduct, even as it expresses our human need for mutuality and humility. Yet the fact that men comprise the major authorial voices in the canon suggests that they do understand the cultural significance of literature.

Preemptively claiming literature for the scrutiny of "rational" criticism has served the privileged position of men. It's prevented literature from having any leveling effect on the general public who, once the dissemination problem was solved by mass printing, had the potential to read socially. In walling off literature from the world of male action, literature instruction has cleverly defused its democratic power to undercut relationships based solely on status. Taming its power to transform, the literature classroom has turned process into commodity and so guaranteed that opportunities for conversation would remain limited. What will it take to see each poem as an entry point for exploring the kinds of disagreement that question all forms of hierarchical control?

To begin with, concentrate deliberately on what is already happening. The reading responses of students can be swamped by both teachers and other students when classroom ground rules encourage domination, competition, and silence. Cleo Cherryholmes' comprehensive checklist allows us to view the verbal environment as a total system:

1. Who is authorized to speak?
2. Who listens?
3. What can be said?
4. What remains unspoken?
5. How does one become authorized to speak?
6. What utterances are rewarded?
7. What utterances are penalized?
8. Which categories, metaphors, modes of descriptions, explanation and argument are valued and praised; which are excluded and silenced?
9. What social and political arrangements reward and deprive statements?
10. Which metaphors, modes of argumentation, explanation, and description are valued?
11. Which ideas are advanced as foundational to the discourse? (Cherryholmes, p. 107)

What interests me about responses to each of these questions is how they help me to distinguish between the discourse of *certainty* and the discourse of *possibility*.

In teasing out the complexity of these contrasting terms, Barbara Danish has been encouraging teachers in New York University's Expository Writing Program to reflect on how what they say opens up spaces for others to join in mutual exploration. Changing the didactic conclusions of "ought to" statements into the inclusive invitations of "what if" statements—replacing "What you are in fact talking about is . . ." with "This is what I heard you say, . . . How does it sound?"—alters the tenor of the dialogue. Through our words we display our respect for what the other knows and feels. By seeing our talk in terms of *possibilities*, rather than *certainties*, we come to understand that the way we speak, as much as what we say, has real consequences for students, who are constantly weighing and choosing among alternative linguistic representations of reality.

Expressing my interpretations—which often begin as prejudices and handed-down beliefs—as conclusions, rather than as options emanating from my thinking in progress, prevents me from creating openings through which others might join the talk and in turn influence me. Reason only prevails when I allow the evidence of others to mingle with my own words and then listen to how these combinations feel inside. This kind of dialogue incorporates the interpretations of others in order to visit previously unexplored territories. To move among openly contested positions, such as what happens when members of a jury try to reach a decision in the presence of contradictory evidence and testimony, I try to encourage mutual discovery and to keep suspended for the moment any final choices that might leave someone unheard. A discourse of possibility keeps reason united with feeling by circling the conversation among all the participants. In this way, the criteria for decision making are held public and continually elaborated, instead of being rendered idiosyncratically.

The complications of conversational competence in the literature classroom suggest that I must consciously coordinate a number of contradictory desires:

1. I'll need confidence in my own initial reading response, while keeping that position permeable and nondogmatic. I must publicly show that my position is open to change by revealing my self-reflections. This becomes difficult because my confidence begins to slip away when I see the limitations of my response. I must try to resist the readings of others until I see my own segue into the conversation.

2. I must be able to listen to the other in ways that are connecting. This means I must imagine the implications of what is being said from the perspective of the person saying it, not just from my own vantage point.

3. I need to find ways of articulating my own position so as to allow it to mesh with the perspectives of others. I must try to find patterns of congruence with the other without losing the core of my own position. To do this I must speak some version of the discourse of possibility.

4. I must be ready to identify discrepancies in my argument and the levels of meaning to which they are related, but this doesn't imply my vacillating in the face of contradiction.

5. Even as I show a willingness to be committed to my emerging position, I need to continue to try to build a more comprehensive and inclusive understanding based on new combinations and further elaborations, rather than simply grasp after some quick formulation.

6. As I recognize that two things cannot occupy the same space, I must be willing not only to compromise, but to articulate exactly what is gained or lost by relinquishing my position. This involves being willing to see opportunities in dialogue and negotiation, not merely losses and defeats. All this commits me to moving beyond the competitive, winner-take-all approach to human encounters.

7. I must try to hold a larger ecological view of any local argument or position that I am holding. I must look for more ab-

stract positions from which any local disagreement or dispute might be illuminated.

8. I must be willing to suspend disbelief, to tolerate ambiguity, and to act as though opposing perspectives can live in some kind of harmony. I acknowledge that criticism can exist without encouraging direct, personal confrontation. This highlights the key reading question in a democracy: Is it really possible to encompass a pluralistic view of human and cultural experience?

Balancing indeterminacy and control while discussing a text develops habits of negotiation. Democratic goals for education will remain elusive unless the school environment actively contributes demonstrable democratic behavior or scripts. These behaviors involve being committed to the kinds of conversational processes that encourage and mediate disagreements. If the reason for sharing our individual responses is not to get immediate confirmation, but to test and improve them, then the talk surrounding a poem can foster the open and unpredictable processes of relationship. In choosing among interpretations and seeing their implications, we celebrate the reflective process. The dance of conversation encourages connectedness and mutuality as opposed to isolation and transmission. How might we engage in the serious play that can make this happen?

Notes

1. Shanker, Albert. 26 June 1988. "Where We Stand." *New York Times,* section 4, p. 7.

2. From Amherst Class of 1965 letter. 16 March 1992.

3. The summary information and the author quotations in this paragraph are contained in Brown and Gilligan, p. 239. See *Works Cited* for specific citations for each study.

Chapter Twelve

Conversational Responses to Poems

Reading as a social act occurs by design, not by accident. To help students understand the value of reading together, teachers work deliberately, focusing on both attitude and procedure. We don't just wait for poems to be read differently in democratic settings; we consciously reflect on how classroom talk and the activities we plan serve to promote a democratic stance toward reading. We attend to the openness of texts as a way of mediating individual novelty with the commonality of mutual understanding. By rendering our own readings vulnerable, we establish that our concerns are inclusive and democratic.

Building on the opportunities of uncertainty and indeterminacy that have been identified by poststructuralism and reader-response criticism, we now see that a lack of closure encourages democratic accessibility. Previously, by acting as though there were final readings for texts, we denied students access to contested readings. When certainty dominates, we lose the joy of being a social reader and a member of a *response*-ible community. By inviting the expression of many perspectives, the teacher of literature promotes equity and mutuality, replaces power with negotiation. It is not easy to develop democratic competence when existing institutions of schooling are mostly concerned with order and control—with sorting people and keeping them apart. Yet, as Dewey and other progressives have shown, every area of the curriculum can be organized democratically in terms of problem solving, active learning, agenda negotiation, and interpersonal cooperation. The reading and writing of literature, however, offers the primary opportunity for developing these social abilities.

The teacher's theory of literary response is crucial in advancing the notion of democratic reading. Unless we're committed to collaborative approaches to textual uncertainty, the poem will only be an occasion for us to display "correct" answers. When this happens, knowledge, which is subsequently fed back on some test, functions to separate and rank students, not to draw out their individual resources collectively. Without a democratic climate in the classroom, little more than literary information is conveyed. A teacher who assumes total command of what students may say in the literature lesson drives the pleasure of the text underground, if it doesn't disappear altogether. Students are naturally curious when it comes to aesthetics and values. The challenge is to exploit this curiosity by both pushing and *trusting* the students, not by infantilizing them. In this sense, one appropriate response to a work of art can often be the creation of some corresponding work of art. This responding text will satisfy to the extent it enriches and pushes forward the human conversation initiated by the original text. Joining with student readers in transactional ways, we help establish in them confidence and security. Then their own readings and interpretations might serve to arouse contact with others.

Democratic values are not just another guise for eclecticism, where the teacher indiscriminately employs any activity that grabs the students' interests. A democratic position is committed to particular ways humans might transact with each other. It fosters ways of knowing that blend multiple perspectives into benevolent communities.

Much of the talk about how literature ennobles our lives, while appearing to be enlightened, is actually deeply undemocratic. Such talk places the message of literature in the text itself, not in the transaction between the text and the social reader. To gain access to this message, readers must rely on specially anointed readers/critics who serve as cultural priests. Accordingly, much literature appreciation teaching is about someone else's appreciation, not the students'. It disallows direct engagement with the literary work and often imparts a sense of despair that literature is irrelevant, something only for "smart" people. Literature does, of course, function in every culture by both reflecting and shaping cultural values and wisdom. However, in a system in which people are trying to live together democratically, the disagreements of social readers serve as a hallmark. Compliant readers, or readers who are certain, diminish the play of literature and so impede the course of democracy.

Keeping the Text in Mind

As a teacher, I hate to admit that I find it stressful to break with traditional patterns of control in the classroom. After mouthing the words *independence* and *self-determination,* I find myself turning around and bristling when the "obvious" response is not forthcoming from students. It's so much easier to lay down the law by offering preemptive readings. Or, attempting to appear more enlightened, I can welcome response, even as I subtly shape it to the "right" view by overpowering with argument and information. Let students display the scattered iron filings of their minds; then I, the all-knowing magnet, properly align them according to my field of force. Maybe I'll never be comfortable in having many disparate readings exit the same lesson at once. But exactly what these disparate readings are I'll never know if I only listen to protect myself.

The open discussions that occur after students read a poem often seem from a world not my own. Many statements are highly judgmental and not what I would see as defensible. As the discussion proceeds, I often find it difficult to hold on to a thread of coherence that indicates some progress in learning and understanding. Faced with this feeling of incomprehension, a number of teacherly strategies might focus the rush of remarks. Not only can I control turn taking, but I can begin to map the contributions according to my own preconceived pattern of understanding. By urging students in particular directions, I can force their contributions to serve in place of my own.

Sometimes there's the direct gambit of exhorting the students back to the text—Where is the evidence for your claim in terms of the author's particular words? This ploy, influenced by the close readings of new criticism, privileges the words on the page. If the students do not somehow get back to the text itself—and the text could be a piece of student writing—what's the point in having the author's words in the room? My secret hope here is that the text itself will reinforce *my* readings, so I won't be annoyed by off-the-mark comments or suddenly find myself aggressively questioning the students, sending them the message that they are not getting the "correct" meaning of the text.

Of course, the text itself doesn't always bring more order or coherence to the discussion. Still, I wonder about talk that appears to distance itself from the actual ink marks on the page. I'd prefer debating interpretation at the site of the author's actual words, rather than amid the ungrounded speculations of our *remembered* readings. But this does not remove my dilemma. It seems I can be guilty of making students toe the line at either site.

One alternative I have experimented with involves *performing* the literary text. Borrowing from protocol or reading-aloud analysis as it's been applied to composing process research, I have students start at the beginning and take turns reading aloud one stanza or paragraph at a time. This is not, however, nonstop reading. The students interrupt themselves as they read, *performing* their inner monologue of questioning, connecting, and meaning making. They comment on what confuses them, how their presuppositions link with an author's statements, how a kind of sense begins to emerge for them as the text unfolds, and how their responses relate to previous readings. There is also room for other students and myself to join in and extend the reflections and complicate the conversation.

What I've found is that the commentary that hovers just over the poem immediately before us differs greatly in quality from the aimless discussions that I'd formerly considered to be free and open. First, it sticks closely to the author's words, and, second, it prevents me from preempting open exploration by obliging me to become a reader of the text alongside the students. In this role, while I may have more experience, more "answers," I am trying, once again, to make fresh sense of the poem just as my students may be doing for the first time. Then, when students begin to feel confident enough to select their own texts for such a class reading, I imagine that together we've taken an important step toward intellectual independence.

Initiating Written Conversations

When I read poems with students, I continually struggle with my equilibrium. I want to find ways to encourage democratic response and dialogue without usurping control of the classroom conversation. I want students talking and involved, yet I don't want to badger them. Too readily I rush in to fill the discussion space that exists to be negotiated between us. Sharing responses in an open conversation, one in which all participants add to and revise their understandings of the texts on the basis of back-and-forth contributions— this obviously requires a tentative stance and a commitment to staying with the process even when at times the results appear muddled.

Such collaborative reading practices feel strange at first. They expose our individual readings as largely indeterminate and uncertain. Students can feel uncomfortable with the unrestricted, give-and-take exploratory talk that I'm expecting of them—indeed, trying to model—and so they have a tendency to be quiet. As they await directions from me, I end up unwittingly assuming the lead in the discussion. But of course this defeats my purpose of having them discover their own intentions, responses, connections. Even as I seek methods to remove the safety net of my teacherly props, students cleverly discover ways of skirting around my constraints. Student classroom maneuvers often seem directed at locating some haven in which they might escape the risks that uncertainty and learning always entail.

On one occasion when I was reading a poem—*one I'd not previously seen*—with a group of four sixteen-year-old girls, I wondered what would happen if we tried conversing with written words rather than spoken words. At the time, I was in England and the poem, which a colleague, Jenifer Smith, had provided, was "Grandmother's Ring" by Kathleen Jamie:

When, in the dark, old-fashioned street
of bungalows, a neighbor enquired
after my Gran, I tried to sound mature
but failed. My ten-years voice splintered
as I summonsed up the words 'she died last night'.

She left me a hideous ring.
It was laid away in velveteen, in some
secret place, to await 'the future'
and forgotten. But, as I breezed
away my teens, something strange occurred:

It transformed like a chrysalis into a butterfly.
(Or perhaps it was I who'd changed?)
We took it out the day of my engagement: It was
exquisite. In the jeweller's shop
where I was scared to cough

my clothes all scruffed, he looked at me
in some disdain, then peered down his inch-long
telescope. And grew excited. Well, as much as such
sombre grey-legs ever dare. He called his student, 'Look,
such rare, perfect colour!' then turned to me, began 'My dear . . .'

She's laughing now. I can see her bloomers
(pink, with frills) wrapped around her laughing thighs.
I can visualise the slant-ceiling
of the attic room where she and I
sat for hours making stories, poems, rhymes:

She left me, too, a love of complicated sounds, and tales
of high adventure. Of musical words,
and made up scraps of nonsense.
So years on, when she had died, and I
was old enough to choose; she made me write.

Not doctor, or teach, or engineer.
And having made sure I'd always be poor,
she left me a ring worth a fortune. Sapphires and diamonds
shoved in my pocket, I walked home,
half-laughing through the pricking tears. How did she know?

The poem provided a moving and fresh recollection of what the poet had inherited from her grandmother. What had originally been considered a worthless ring turns out to be quite valuable, but such a worldly possession is contrasted to a love of language that is really the grandmother's more lasting legacy. Surely this poem would prompt these girls into responding.

Normally, as a way in, I would have "tried on" this poem by reading it several times, before asking the students to do likewise—a common enough teacher practice, one that focuses the class, catches our attention, and suspends the rush toward interpretation and judgment. But, as I explained to the girls—Kari, Tara, Glenda, and Melinda—we were just going to read and write to ourselves for awhile before talking: "Read the poem silently to yourself and in the margins begin writing any impressions or responses that come to you." Part of this writing, I assumed, might just include free associations. They could jot down brief comments, phrases, or questions at any point in their reading and at the end might begin a longer, open response. But these directions grew out of my trained expectations about how one should proceed as a reader; the girls initially showed little sense of how to proceed.

As the five of us began writing responses on the copies of the poem I'd distributed, I could see that they seemed hesitant. Their eyes moved from the poem to sneaking glances at each other, as if waiting for some signal that would tell them what to write. Perhaps the first responses they wrote down were so halting because they were working with someone unfamiliar. Here I was, an American teacher who they'd met only that morning. This alone could have been enough to dampen their enthusiasm for exploring possible connections between themselves and the poem. Raising questions might expose their ignorance, make them appear inept and inadequate. Intrepidly, however, I kept scribbling away, making a mess of my page by including arrows and circles and writing a series of impressions and questions. At the bottom I wrote a brief comment that connected my own experience to the relationship being explored by the poem:

I never had close relationships with my grandparents but the story my mum tells about her grandmother seems to apply here. She tells endless stories of how my great-grandmother had such a zest for life and how this carried over to her. I wonder how we do inherit these traits and how in this poem the gift of language being passed on contrasts in an important way with the seeming insignificance of the ring.

Eventually, the girls began to put down more comments, but after about fifteen minutes, everyone seemed to run out of steam. It would then have been an obvious time to share our individual responses in open discussion. The moment, however, didn't yet seem right for talk. I felt that the girls, given what I could glance from their papers, had only scratched the surface. If we immediately began talking, once again I might end up overpowering the discussion, however indirectly, and the deeper range of responses that they might be feeling would be lost forever.

So I made up something new on the spot, a variation of note passing in class. I asked them to pass what they'd written along to the next person. Then, continuing our vow of silence, we'd respond in writing to the just-written responses still fresh on the page. Next, we'd keep circulating these papers until everyone had at least one chance to respond to each set of marginalia. Such a written conversation might cut back on my dominant presence as teacher. By remaining silent, I hoped they would feel safe to work with the words that others were writing and not be immediately thrust into the performance mode of discussion.

Everyone passed their paper to the right and followed my directive to continue commenting on what was already written there— extending, questioning, elaborating, contradicting. This at first went slowly because the girls felt unsure of what was going on. Soon, however, they joined in the flow of this note passing, and we kept exchanging papers until each contained extensive marginalia from five hands. By then, each of us was anxious to see what conversations had been carried out on our original papers.

Having granted the girls and myself this extra freedom to explore the poem, I was pleased to observe what I took to be an important shift occurring for them. They began to move from using a conventional mode of literary explication, one that offered generalized *meanings* and focused on the formal aspects of how the poem was working, to considering the poem's significance for their own lives. This didn't mean that these lines of verse were merely an occasion for discussing relationships with grandparents, but, once the girls felt more comfortable exploring these emotions, their stories of opportunity and regret began to surface.

This shift to a deeper level of understanding (many teachers, of course, regard making personal associations as the more *superficial* level) is reflected in what Tara wrote just before we began our discussion: "I did not have a close relationship with my grandfather and now he is dead all I have is a photo and his train set. He had so much to teach me but I was never there to learn. The poem makes me remember and wish I had done more."[1] Her comment was prompted by reading what I'd written about my own relationship to my grandparents (quoted earlier). I found this contrasted in an important way with the initial response she'd written at the beginning of our session. There, she'd kept personal matters at a safe distance by generalizing and using the language of abstraction: "The poem is very fast. It shows how age can change your view of things and how people that have passed away are never forgotten. It tries to tell us how love can be so difficult and complicated in different ways." This way of responding suggests that poetry is supposed to teach the reader a lesson, and, to be sure, in this instance the lesson for her includes some important sentiments. I read Tara's words as being safely poised between the abstract and the personal, written as they are in the prose of the impersonal literary essay. I wondered what experiences in Tara's life had given rise to such propositions.

Under Tara's comment I'd written, "I wonder if this is true of all people; so what makes the difference?" Glenda in turn replied to my query, "I think if they were special to you they will always have a very special, moving part of your memories." I then came back with, "What makes her [the grandmother] special?" From my perspective, Tara had set off a chain of thoughts well worth exploring, but such a chain remained incomplete without the events and incidents that comprised the actual lives of these students. Sooner or later, I surmised, we'd have to consider our own grandparents or at least our relationships with old people, who may be held only in memory, if this poem was truly going to resonate for us.

As the written conversation evolved, it became clear that, because I had no ready answers as to the poem's "true" meaning and was ready to sanction personal stories, the girls had convened and entered *their* interrogation of the poem, not mine. By passing notes, they saw it was safe to correct me by continuing a conversation in the margins, one that was no longer marginalized. This allowed us to be both playful and serious with our remarks. When Melinda wrote on her paper, "Gran lingers on in the attic," I pictured a creepy image and so responded, "Sounds like a Friday the 13th movie." Melinda's remark, however, led Tara in a different direction: "Yes, I agree the attic will always bring back Gran." Finally, after Melinda's paper circled back to me a second time, I wrote next to Tara's words, "memories triggered off by association."

On Tara's paper this back-and-forth writing can be seen starting with her comment, "From age ten to teens, very fast moving." Next to this I noted, "The notion of fast-moving didn't occur to me at all." She then came back with, "In years not in motion!"—a misreading of my careless handwriting? At a later point she wrote, "Her age made the ring change in a visual aspect." I then added, "which translates into a monetary aspect," and she concluded, "Yes!"

Another conversational chain was begun by Glenda. Next to the line in the poem, "(Or perhaps it was I who'd changed)," she declared, "I don't think that line should be there. The line before was far too special to be followed by that." This clearly was a strong response on Glenda's part for on another paper she wrote once again, "I didn't like this line which followed such a great meaning line before." Tara took an opposing position, "I don't agree, it was her who had changed, not the ring," as did Melinda, "I disagree, strongly!!!, it is a sudden afterthought, a realization that she is a child no more." And finally, Kari lent her support to both these objections: "I agree!" before I tagged on, "I wonder if I could get it without the parenthesis." With such a disagreement firmly located in the margins, we could return in our subsequent discussion and explore further the competing readings of this line.

On an earlier line of the poem, "to await 'the future'," Glenda's gloss, "like the ring her memories had to 'await the future'," drew further, expanding remarks by the other girls. First Melinda added, "Maybe she needed time to accept that 'gran' was gone, maybe she needed to make a break." This led Tara to confirm assertively Melinda's more tentative query, "She did need time to accept her Grandmother's death." Finally, Kari offered a more elaborate extension of what Glenda had started, "Yes, I agree. But I don't think she wanted to deal with it straight away. And the ring symbolises this. It's put away, not to be looked at again until she is a lot older. (I'm not sure if that makes sense!)"

It does, of course, make perfect sense and shows how a particular conversational chain written out in this fashion can lead a reader to develop an understanding by building on a theme or question initiated by others. We'll never know whether, independent of this written conversation, Kari would have made such an association between the time a person needs to adjust to a death and the ring being put away. On this occasion at least, working on the poem silently in concert with others seemed to prompt and push the girls beyond the first comments they'd made independently.

In many instances, once a line of thought was opened, most of us felt compelled to throw in our own reactions. Kari opened her paper with, "It's a sad poem. I would imagine Grans was a very fun loving lady. The girl was very close to her." Melinda added, "I don't think Gran would want to be remembered sad." I chimed in with, "I don't see it as a sad poem" and then promptly added, "So we need to resolve the 'evidence'?" Tara then rounded off this chain with, "moving maybe, sad?" Here was something we could pursue later, wondering about whether poems are sad or readers bring sadness to them.

Many questions were asked as we wrote in the margins, and sometimes a hesitant answer appeared. Kari: "Why should she sound mature?" Tara: "It can sound mature to try and cope with her loss?" Then I responded, but ended with my own question, "I guess this is from the point of view that as children sometimes we wanted to act 'grown-up' because we're practicing playacting. I want to know why she thinks she failed or 'what is mature behavior at this point?'" Next to the phrase, "my clothes all scruffed," I wrote, "Why this line?" Tara helped me out with, "Maybe its because she had never been rich and wanted to express this in her poem," and Melinda added, "It is the little ten yr old school girl."

There was much point and counterpoint at the surface reading level as we played with individual lines and meanings. Similarly, the written conversation revealed a split among the girls at the deeper level of what the poem signified for each of them. Three of them talked about how the poem moved them. The emotional connection in each instance involved being drawn back to thoughts about how their grandparents figured importantly in their lives. As Melinda wrote, "It is a very touching poem, though it is about good things, it is ringed with sadness, it also symbolises change, the way in which somebody you knew long ago, comes back and is unrecognisable and you think—is it really them?"

In contrast, Kari admitted to a different story. Melinda had written first: "When I was about 7 my grandfather died. All I remember was a fat jolly man sitting by the fire rocking me on his knee. My gran lives with us now. My other grandfather I don't know his name & I have never seen him. I think the poem in a way symbolises lost treasure, a longing to know." But Kari showed how her underlying experience had led her to receive the poem in a quite different way: "I'm not close to any of my grandparents and I'm lucky enough to have all of them with me. I feel guilty when I see that others wish that they could know them better, but they don't have the chance and I do. I'm taking them for granted and I need to change this." In exploring these differences the girls quickly appreciated how the circumstances of life contribute powerfully to the stances we take as readers. Here the poem was also suggesting to Kari that there might be another way to live a relationship.

The whole emotional dimension of the poetic responses displayed by these girls, including the layers of Kari's disagreement, only surfaced because I was able to stay out of the way as a teacher long enough for it to develop. In joining the circle of response, my presence obviously set a tone, but finally all of our voices were being celebrated in both the margin commentary and the discussion that followed. By writing our responses within the network of a conversation, Tara, Melinda, Glenda, Kari, and I were able to create a spell of equality that helped us see layers of the poem we might otherwise not have noticed.

Variations on a Theme

Buoyed by the success of this experiment,[2] I have since tried any number of variations using writing in the margins to slow down and make more deliberate and more open the process of responding to poems. Much of the time, readers can be so caught up with what they want to say that they leave little room to take in the perspective of others. This tendency to show off one's individual wares seems best disrupted in small groups, where more informality and less competition prevail.

In one class of university students, I shuffled the deck by giving groups two versions of the same poem. The different copies were interspersed in each pile of six that I handed to the groups, so no one knew they weren't all getting the same version. Every student immediately began reading and then gradually wrote some marginalia. At some point, after they made the first exchange of papers, the discovery came; but not everyone had the same experience of recognizing the different versions. In some instances, students had written on the back of the sheet, so the next person failed to look at the poem again and, assuming it was the same version, quickly began to write an answering response. Eventually, despite the vow of silence, someone shouted out, "Hey, these aren't the same poem!" Yet, rather than feel betrayed, the students attended even more closely to the language of the poem as they worked to sort out the two versions and their preferences.

In part, this heightened involvement had been my intention, but such directives are better coming from the students themselves. While each version of the poem I used in that class had been written by the same author, either the teacher or students can create other drafts for consideration in this way by the small groups. The versions might be radically different, or perhaps there will only be subtle shifts in wording or phrasing that might, at first, go undetected. The point is not so much to finely tune a student's sense of literary form, as it is to keep her being a contributor, not just an expropriator, when it comes to talking about her reading of literary texts. Indeed, many students themselves begin to select poems for discussion, once they discover that the classroom forum exists to serve *their* purposes.

On another occasion I gave each of the six group members a separate poem from *Counterpoint,* a collection by R. S. Thomas. These poems had been specifically arranged by Thomas to open a sequence of short religious meditations he'd entitled "BC." The first poem contains passages like,

> If you can imagine a brow puckered
> before thought, Imagine this page
> immaculately conceived
> in the first tree, with man rising
> from all fours endlessly to begin
> puckering it with his language.
>
> (p. 8)

In this vein, the last sentence of the sixth poem reads,

> ". . . Wiser
> the Buddha who, though he looked
> long, had no name for the packed
> bud never to become a flower.
>
> (p. 13)

Thomas appeared, to me, to be thinking in terms of some global historical development, but the clues were subtle at best. I wondered in what kind of sequence readers would place these poems if they originally came upon them in no particular order, and what kinds of arguments they would choose to justify their selections. So I asked the groups of graduate students to hammer out some kind of consensus regarding what sequence worked best for them.

Normally they would have been able to pass the poems around and make individual choices before trying to negotiate a group decision. However, always on the lookout for a new wrinkle to push the students into collective autonomy, I asked them not to let anyone else see their sheets. Instead, they could only read their individual poems aloud, letting them be taken in solely through the other members' ears. This caused quite a stir, but it awakened in them a deeper sense of the importance of sound and repetition in poetry.

Thus all members read the poem they had been given numerous times to the rest of the group in order that everyone might have access to it.

I was amazed at how they stuck with this, reading orally, over and over, and discovering in the process that reading well took some conscious effort. Still, with each reading came improvement in rhythm, pacing, and emphasis, along with an increased commitment to the poem they were reading. Each reading was interspersed with some commentary. The students who were listening intently occasionally wrote down a phrase or two, but mostly they showed a concentrated effort in staying with the sound of the words as the words began to fall into a discernible pattern from poem to poem. In negotiating an order for the poems, the students began to discover how words and themes connected across the poems. Somehow, the reading repetitions placed the individual poems in their heads in a way that doesn't seem to happen when we look at the printed page only with our eyes and not our ears. I gave the students almost an hour for this activity. Nevertheless, at the end of class when I left, one group was still going strong. What mysteries in their own responses had each student at last been authorized to discover?

Notes

1. The written conversation cited in the following pages is reprinted with the permission of all participants.

2. I note here my debt to the extensive poetry discussion work that Patrick Dias has carried out in classrooms. He has demonstrated that even young students, without teacher interference, are perfectly capable of creating their own productive agendas when it comes to poetry (see Dias, 1987).

Chapter Thirteen

Conversing About Literature Without a Teacher

For most of our lives, the conversations in which we participate do not include teachers. To discover the kind of social conversation that might ensue when adults write together in response to a poem, I gathered four experienced readers to read a poem they'd not seen previously. Because I would be absent from their written conversation, I'd left the four of them with copies of the poem, unidentified by author. I'd copied the poem on the middle of oversized paper— 25½ inches × 14 inches. This provided ample margin space for their written responses. I encouraged any kind of marking—underlining, arrows, question marks, single words or phrases, longer comments or queries, and so forth. They could go back through the poem as often as they wanted, relating whatever was occurring to them, including questions, interpretations, and connections to their personal experience or to other works of art. The key, however, was to resist talking among themselves until they felt finished with their written conversation.

When they came to a resting place with their initial response writing, they were to exchange papers with someone else and continue with their written responses, now circling between the poem and their accumulating marginalia. This exchange process was to be repeated until, minimally, each reader had marked something on everyone else's copy. They could, of course, return to any copy more than once, depending on the written conversation that seemed to be developing. How long this would take wasn't clear; I just asked them to follow these procedures until they entered a comfortable rhythm of sharing their written responses with each other. The poem I gave them was "First Gestures" by Julia Kasdorf:

Among the first we learn is goodbye,
a tiny wrist between Dad's forefinger
and thumb forced to wave bye-bye to Mom,
whose hand sails brightly behind a windshield.
Then it's done to make us follow:
in a crowded mall, a woman waves, "Bye,
we're leaving," and the boy stands firm
sobbing, until at last he runs after her
among shoppers drifting by like sharks
who must drag their great hulks
underwater, even in sleep, or drown.

Living, we cover vast territories;
imagine your life drawn on a map—
a scribble on the town where you grew up,
each bus trip traced between school
and home, or a clean line across the sea
to a place you flew once. Think of the time
and things we accumulate, all the while growing
more conscious of losing and leaving. Aging,
our bodies collect wrinkles and scars
for each place the world would not give
under our own weight; our thoughts get
laced with strange aches, sweet as the final
chord that hangs in a guitar's blond torso.

Think how a particular ridge of hills
from a summer of your childhood grows
in significance, or one hour of light—
late afternoon, say, when thick sun flings
the shadow of Virginia creeper vines
across the wall of a tiny, white room
where a woman makes love for the first time.
Its leaves tremble like small hands
against the screen, while she sobs
in the arms of a bewildered man, too young
to see that as we gather losses
we may also grow in love—
as in passion, the body shudders
and clutches what it must release.

Their written conversation lasted close to an hour, though the participants—Hester and Alex, who were working on doctorates in English, and Doreen and Andreas, who were working on doctorates in English education—reported they could easily have spent double the time if they hadn't had previous commitments.[1] The marginalia were rich and multifaceted, but presenting their written words in sequential fashion fails to capture the participants' reported experience of feeling freer and freer as they went along. They also described their written exchanges as being circular, as yielding a sense of "all at onceness"—something difficult to render in any linear transcript. Their written conversation did reveal, however, that their readings grew more complex and satisfying as a result of being part of a social venture. Beginning with their own insights, they reached out in tentative and nondogmatic ways to incorporate and build on each other's responses. By combining all the strands into an ongoing inquiry, we see the democratic play enjoyed by these four readers.

As expected, the beginning point of this democratic conversation is a continual attempt to just make sense of the unfamiliar text. Doreen, for instance, tries to piece together line 5. "What's the antecedent—What's done to 'make us follow'? Why the colon after that?" Then associating the wave with "underwater" (line 11) she continues her questioning: "Is it the wave that makes us follow? Wave as seduction?" At the very end of the poem, Andreas asks, "What must be released?" and, trying to sort out images between the first and last stanzas, wonders, "Boy firm / leaves (woman?) trembling (sobbing?) Is the firm boy now bewildered man?" These questions, as ways into the poem, also engage the readers in considering their own understandings of human behavior. The very first line provokes Doreen to write, "They teach us to say goodbye—no—we *learn* it." This triggers Alex to respond, "What do we learn? To replace our feeling of loss with a gesture. Here, if anywhere, is a place where the world refuses to give way, the sweep of our arm is the first line." Finally, Andreas offers this rejoinder: "Hey—I'm not sure here—We learn a *gesture*, social meaning is constructed around that gesture, we repeat it, it sounds like I'm a behaviorist here—Is it one or the other? Are we taught and do we learn consciously?"

In this mutual exploration, the readers imagine themselves within the events of the first stanza and take account of their feelings. Hester detects a "hint of violence" in lines 2–3, and Alex agrees, "For some weird reason I feel nervous about this image— like the baby's wrist will be crushed." But Andreas expresses an opposite feeling, "Hmm—I felt safe here—as if being guided and held securely!" Doreen, on the other hand, joins the majority when she adds, "But it's about *force*—not safe for me." Further, she notes that "The separation is forced" (lines 6–7), to which Alex adds, "Forced to leave the mother. From this comes the bewilderment—

which is just another way of *refusing*, then, to be there for her." This in turn gets Alex wondering about the father's role in this departure. "Why isn't Dad more implicated? Why doesn't he do something? Or do we take away from the mother the power to separate from us— while we also blame her for it."

For Andreas, however, Alex's question leads nowhere: "Implicated in what, I wonder?" But Andreas does wonder about the word "Mom" when he writes, "Why not Mommy? Softer. *Mom* tough on the lips, not *mn . . . mom*—closed mouth, tight lipped utterance with a gasping center." The concern here is very much about families, about the mother and father relationship and their responsibility for the child. Hester joins in, "Yes! The father is urging this separation from the mother—jealous? (Sorry, I can't help it—I've been trying not to be reductively Freudian—but there you are.)" She is then supported by Doreen, who connects the mother in the first stanza to the woman in the third, "Yes—and both times it's the woman who leaves—named Mom in one place, woman in another."

There is much agitated response to the shark image. Andreas notes, "Not something I would associate with shoppers." But Alex does try to connect the image to the place: "Except maybe at xmas when you need to hold your breath just to be able to stomach another trip to the mall." Despite this interpretive move, Hester remains dissatisfied. "Why sharks—who perceives them as dangerous—author, boy, woman?" Alex confesses that he "actually forgot the danger. Maybe it was because they seemed lumbering, like shoppers. My guess is that they're like boys, bewildered but possessing sharp teeth." Hester extends the image but doesn't reverse its feeling of danger, "cave of the sleeping sharks in Mexico—nurse sharks, fairly benign, but still ominous." And she wonders, "What does underwater mean to the shoppers?"

Next, Andreas, who used to work in New York's financial district, makes a personal connection to the sharks: "Evokes images of Wall Street for me—less an image of dragging heaviness/ more an image of a slow, deliberate search for prey, search for nourishment for 'their great hulks'—not plodding, perhaps appearing to drift, but more likely plotting." Finally, Hester makes a key remark about perspective: "Why the strange union of a terrifying animal and an unwieldy, lumbering, almost stupidly benign mindlessness? Is this how children think of grown-ups?" which Andreas confirms as a "Great question! I'm inclined to think so." Alex then connects the closing lines of this stanza to another text. "What do the shoppers drag themselves under? The misery of being alienated from the means of production? Makes me think of *1984*, gray people with dust in their pores lumbering along, as if in sleep, but a dreamless sleep, that you wake from feeling tired and lumpy." And Doreen adds a coda: "And underwater—dragging—moving slowly."

The second stanza exposes two fault lines for the readers: the image of the map and the contrast between a poetry of abstract ideas and a poetry of narrative presence. Andreas expresses his appreciation of the speculative ideas of the second stanza. "I like the shift here—it sucks me into the poem." But Doreen disagrees, "Somehow this stanza pushes me away." To which Alex jokes, knowing well Doreen's preferences, "Because there's no story in it." Then Hester gives a reason why she likes the second stanza. "Funny, I liked this stanza best—maybe because it seemed the least gendered. Also the least claustrophobic—movement outwards, solitary." She sees the map as a dynamic image pointing to lines 15–16. "For some reason this is a really satisfying image to me. Visual evidence of your existence marked on a communal document, the tracing of lines repeated representing a span of time, but captured all at once symbolically on the paper." This contribution leads Alex to write, "Traced now makes me think of taking the pattern from someone else—the only way I used to be able to draw." To which Andreas adds a humorous personal touch, "Still the only way I do!"

The map metaphor is felt by Doreen to be a constraining image: "Cover up?" But Hester responds to her by pushing in the opposite direction. First, she confirms Doreen's reading. "Interesting that you see it as covering up and I saw it more as revealing." Then she goes on to negotiate the gap between the two responses. "Although actually my satisfaction and your dissatisfaction seem related—it's a very . . . I can't think of the word—almost capitalist metaphor. Possession. Marking your territory by urinating like (male) animals. The Western Territories, conquering the West." This fronting of the gender agenda causes Alex to speculate, "Interesting—mapping as a capitalist. Maps do come with the accumulation of sufficient capital for mercantilist ventures. If men mark a place, they also describe women as already marked—having a scent." This, however, cues Doreen's issue about power and agency, and so she writes of the map, "Who draws it? The map is two dimensional—I don't want to imagine my life drawn on a map." Finally, there is a gender split regarding the torso in the stanza's concluding line. Hester identifies this as a "woman," but Alex argues, "man. blond has no 'e.' (I realize that's French, but it's how I read it, like a blond young man.)"

This split foreshadows the final disagreements, as the four readers position their own histories in relation to the love-making event of the concluding stanza. Who are these two figures in terms of age, experience, power? How does gender pull us back to what the boy is learning about gestures at the beginning of the poem? Doreen focuses on *who* fails to do the seeing in line 35: "Does the woman see? The man is too young to see—but is the woman? Maybe—yes—I think she is too young to see—maybe not, there's only one comma." Then she wonders about the loss. "Always—the loss of reaching the top—of going over the top?" Meanwhile, the men are seeing a clear age split between the man and the woman. Next to the first stanza, Alex writes, "Again, like below, the woman is wise, the boy young. She makes up here for the crying she'll do later. The bewilderment that protects him below makes him impotent here." Andreas comments, "—Yes, but she seems more vulnerable (to me). She seems to have no agency here—he is bewildered, she sobs—what (else) is she feeling? Thinking? Doing? She's 'in the arms of . . .' Engulfed, Overwhelmed?" And Hester, continuing to employ her economic metaphor, wonders, "Possessed? How can the young man imagine the thoughts of the woman who is primarily a possession?" To which Alex replies, "No—he doesn't have thoughts—so why should she? Or, rather, his thoughts are to himself—why would this make her cry?"

There is a sense of the erotic here that generates a response from the men. Andreas writes next to the beginning of the third stanza, "Very Sexual Imagery." This gets Alex thinking, "Wow, I like that. I hadn't seen it and now it seems more fun. To me there's a playfulness in remembering that kind of ridge that contrasts with the weeping about to come. But maybe that's because I'm a boy." Then Doreen, wanting to find her own gender firmly inscribed in the poem, forcefully responds to Alex with, "—A boy? I'm not sure what I want to say about that. It makes me go back to the poem to look for the word 'girl'—because I know the word 'man' is in the poem." In her usual fashion, Hester moves to a mediated position of abstraction: "Men are narrative constructions and have different ages; 'women' are a constant."

Later on, Andreas makes a partial underline in *Virgin*ia and draws an arrow to "make love." This provokes another connection Alex had not been alert to, "I didn't get the pun either. Now I see the vine as also trembling. Where's the boy? Where's his imagery? Now I see 'grow' [line 36] as part of the metaphor. But it hasn't felt much like growing to me—it's seemed more depressing and bleak. Well, not bleak, but vacated. Like *Gone with the Wind*—a sad shadow. (All that Southern imagery from one word.)" Doreen then picks up on Alex's use of the word vacated. "This seems really interesting to me—vacated—she's gone—no one is there?" which provokes Alex to respond, "More like she's still there, but now the presence of the place is gone. It's governing spirit has been slain."

As the readers concentrate on the room where the love making occurs, they cultivate a number of associations. Doreen writes, "Tiny—no space; white—no color—I can see the vines—*creeper* vines; creepy, shudders." Then Hester extensively expands on her own associations, "It made me think of a hospital. I have this persistent sense that this stanza is really about childbirth—all that tinyness and smallness, the white room, the sobbing woman, the man clueless as to how to help her, 'gather losses/grow in love'—birth, separation, 'the body shudders and clutches what it must release.' I read that as a sexual metaphor but I don't much like it—I'm more interested in how the young man is like a baby now—circling back to the first stanza." Alex had not seen the connection between the vines and "shudders" so he now responds to Doreen, "I wasn't reading them this way, but now the female does seem to be sneaking back up on the boy she threatened to abandon. She should have just stayed." But this comment about the female having left brings an incredulous rejoinder from Hester. "What?! She left him?"

Alex objects to the tears at the end: "For me, it doesn't have to be this way. The woman, too, can be too young. I don't like this part. It seems to traffic in a frustrating old idea of women as natural wisdom." To which first Hester writes, "I'm glad you don't like it." And then Doreen writes, "So am I." Andreas concludes by moving close to his own life, "Loss as opportunity? Love needs Pain? As I see this for a second time, I am uncomfortable with the images evoked—the context of my life now—the pain I am going through, the adjustments . . ." And then he writes next to the final line, "A Gesture."

Gradually, interpretations take shape as the poem is seen as a totality, and likes and dislikes are more firmly articulated. Alex, for instance, relates "First Gestures" to a poem by Robert Lowell. "The movement of this poem is now reminding me a little of 'Skunk Hour.' But 'SH' seems to get closer to a place of renewal. This poem is nostalgic throughout, and while it sort of gracefully acknowledges the physicality at the end, it doesn't have the integrity of skunks (rats) nosing in the garbage—I see that as a brave, fruitful image. 'SH' is more melodramatic, but even so, for me, more satisfying."

The larger perspective also raises the question of authorship. Hester comments, "Maybe I'm *totally* wrong, but I feel convinced that the writer is a man—the baby at the beginning, the boy in the mall, the young man at the end. There seems to be an analogy between the woman and the baby I don't like very much." Alex offers his support for this thesis: "I agree. It's a man and I don't really like it. Or it's a woman—like James Tiptree [she/he, a woman science fiction writer writing as a man]. It seems like the poor boy is always at other people's command—except who ends up crying?" This query brings the gender discussion full circle as Doreen responds, "I wasn't sure if the baby was a girl or boy—and I'm not sure how you see the analogy. I'm looking to see—what I see is that it is the 'woman who makes love for the first time'—ah—maybe there is that connection to the first line— 'Among the first . . .'" Finally, Andreas adds, "And I read the baby as a boy, too. Though now the violence seen by others in the father's gesture points me to the baby being a girl. But this shifts for me, and I see the baby as a boy—in the same stanza 'the boy stands firm'— seems to point to the same child on a later stage."

What the readers wrote in conversation with each other comes to no conclusion, and this very openness signifies to me that reading as a social act encourages us to tolerate ambiguity and uncertainty. As Doreen commented later on the experience, "I had a sense of how free we were to move any place we wanted; to explore with others, not alone—there was no map here—one layer at a time." By not attempting to determine a poem's meaning absolutely, the readers stay in relationship, both with the poem and with their co-readers.

The Poet Responds

In the case of this poem, the poet, Julia Kasdorf, was available to reflect on the written conversation as it related to her intentions and her sense of revision. Her remarks[2] offer a further example of the textured layers of meaning and significance that surround the conversation that readers enter when they read socially.

Regarding the tension between narrative and exposition, Julia related her particular experience of poetic influence:

> This other poet (object/subject of the poem) and his professional and artistic ambition posed some sort of challenge at the time, just before the publication of my first book, when I was doubting the value of the narrative/domestic/ethnic poetry I'd been writing—all things that have been called "small." I wanted to write a "large" poem, although I was entirely conscious of the tradition and values that reinforce this notion, a tradition I'd resisted even before I could reduce its complexity by "naming" it. Of course I knew better than to be upset by that tradition, yet I was, perhaps as a way of expressing my publication anxiety and fear of failure.

For Julia, this poem served to widen the scope of concerns that she might entertain as a poet:

So I suppose this could be viewed as a persona piece, a trying on of another perspective, resistance and adoration in near equal parts, responding to another in his terms. The tone turned out to be one I like, and I do not see it as an erasure of my voice, but a testing of my own range. I think this may be an important poem for me in the end, partly because of what I learned about writing and the possibilities that can come of conflict and collusion.

The poem satisfies her because "it represents another place from which to work."

Julia had not fully anticipated what readers might discover in this poem. She was "troubled by the violence people found, the mean gender politics, which may be there," though previously she'd not been aware of it because she had not consciously intended it. The poem, however, acts as a story: the writer can never completely control its meaning, which continues to bleed out of the form. Reflecting on the readers' comments did lead Julia to consider, briefly, a revision. First, she wondered, "The fact that I'm both attached to the sharks and bothered by them makes me think they should go. The image may be too weird on one hand and too obvious on another—shoppers sleep-walking, the persistence of life's narrative." But later she concluded, "I feel more confident about the sharks, sinister as they are." The readers also alerted her to a confusion in line 35, which she feels she must clear up:

> *She* is too young, not he. This was my intention, although I see the line is not punctuated or structured to communicate this. This shift, I think, makes a great difference in the poem's effect. And another draft has the woman weeping in the last line, rather than sobbing, which is probably a better choice.

By not allowing poems to be sacred objects, such dialogues enact the virtues of democratic permeability, without sacrificing integrity—not the reader's, not the poet's.

Reading, Time, and Democracy

The central characteristic that I discovered about these evolving written conversations was their *temporal* quality. As Rosenblatt tells us, the poem is best "thought of as an event in time" (Rosenblatt, 1978, p. 12). While it may appear to be happening all at once, reading, and our social talk about it, *exists in time*—both the time it actually takes to complete a single reading and the longer stretch of time in which our original interpretations expand or change.

In the first case, for instance, we may take days to finish a work such as a novel. For no matter how compelling the story may be, our lives are filled with all kinds of events that interrupt our reading. And when we come back to a text, our mood has sometimes shifted or new connections have been made in our mind. Further, even within the boundaries of shorter works, our responses and understandings will shift as we take in new information or as different associations suddenly occur to us. Similarly, our experience with a text over time will never be quite the same, because the conditions and perspectives of our lives change. *The Adventures of Huckleberry Finn* has served as an exciting adventure story for children, but bores many high school students forced to read it. Then, miraculously, it returns as a great American novel under the microscope of college English professors, who help us frame the language and the plot in ways that resonate below the surface of things. In each case, when our position toward the text is altered, then our reading too must be altered—that is if we are to maintain some coherent sense of meaning—and these shifts will be very much influenced by how we share our opinions with others.

This temporal aspect of reading cannot be overemphasized. Time and its changes give democracy the distinction of being an ongoing experiment with its citizens open to new experience and to new evidence. Democracy resists the urge to determine results in advance; it does not freeze time. When we keep our readings tied to time, we learn the importance of permeability in our lives. We learn how to stay with processes still in the making. Thus, we need to listen when Steven Mailloux warns us, "By neglecting the temporal reading process . . . traditional holistic criticism not only distorts the actual effects literature produces; it also omits an important part of the author's intention and artistic technique" (Mailloux, 1982, p. 71). Reading as a social act of meaning building and mutual exchange mirrors the democratic enterprise itself, so we need to be cautious of classroom practices that set poems outside of time by neglecting personal response and dictating final interpretations.

Valuing Small Groups

The readers' words that have come to revolve around "Grandmother's Ring" and "First Gestures" have convinced me that literature classes are best structured democratically around this kind of small-group work. Building on the talk that occurs there, I have observed that student response is different when everyone returns to the large group, a public space where it's usually harder to appear reflective and tentative. While often students feel uncomfortable speaking before a larger audience, they are more involved, even when silent, if just previously they've been active participants in some small group. Also, I find teacher talk is more responsive to concerns that have been percolating up from written conversations. I can remark on activities and experiences as they're developing, rather than just repeat some lesson rehearsed at an earlier time. Teaching literature democratically requires balancing a rough plan with an ongoing improvised conversation—no plan and it's all confusion, all plan and it's a straitjacket. Using small groups gives me license to repeat student responses that I overhear in monitoring the class, and it allows me to reflect openly on how, together, we're making up things as we go along.

When a group seems stalled, I intrude with additional questions and observations to get them going again. Often these brief encounters lead to explicit conversation about group process. People share feelings of vulnerability and discuss how what is being said affects them. Andreas, for instance, indicated later that he had initially felt self-conscious, wondering if his responses would live up to the expectations of the others, whom he felt to be superior readers. This natural feeling of anxiety caused him to make very constrained and brief responses on his initial copy of the poem. But then, as he joined the flow and felt less threatened, his offerings became freer and more self-reflective—it was safe for him to be vulnerable. In general, students have reported that writing first (holding a written conversation) sets up a zone of politeness and protection. They then come to feel secure enough to fully express their disagreements.

Talk about process is not accidental. To practice democratic relationships, to become sensitive to the process of social reading, requires constant attention of a conscious sort. Thus, periodically, each small group chooses one or two observers who, during the discussion, sit back and record the patterns of group interaction. Later they lead the group in a critical but caring consideration of its process. When students learn to work on a poem collaboratively, what I have to say forms a link with what they've been considering. How might these links, based on what students already know, further strengthen their growing confidence as readers?

Notes

1. The following written conversation is presented here with the permission of its authors.

2. Julia Kasdorf's remarks are reprinted here with her permission.

Chapter Fourteen

A Democracy of Readers
and Readings

Inside a display case located in the King's Library at the British Museum lies an opened copy of a book written by Boethius, *De Consolatione Philosophie,* published in 1491. The reason it's on exhibit, surprisingly, has nothing to do with the author. The interest is focused entirely on a reader, who had boldly inked in a fanciful calligraphic drawing of some mythic female figure. This graffito, extending up the outer margin of the left-hand page, testifies to the fact that at some time, in some place, a reader allowed his concentration to wander. The rigors and consolations of philosophy, apparently, didn't inspire the proper respect in the mind of this solitary reader. He instead chose to relate to the book in an unauthorized fashion.

The display case, labeled "Books and their Users," contains a note of explanation that, while trying to be humorous, cannot hide its displeasure at this reader's delinquency: "Dialogue with Books: A Schoolboy's Inattention." The open page is being offered as one early example of how the book-owner relationship might even extend to "pointed indifference to the contents." The moral is plain: No temptress should stand between a scholar, however bored, and his duty. Such discrepancies reveal, however, that authentic personal response only begins when readers are not officially controlled. By tapping a reader's rich internal conversation and set of feelings, and not the orderly version faked for the teacher, we begin to foster her confidence in joining wider circles of conversation.

Having, for so many centuries, taken for granted the easily accessible printed text, we have forgotten how this technology profoundly influenced the prerogatives of the reader. By making possible a new kind of textual ownership, the printing press also led to the personal appropriation of texts. Tediously copied manuscripts had been rare and even sacred objects. Institutions generally owned them, not individuals, and so they were never lightly discarded. Printing made books available on a much wider basis, and this gradually led to the development of a more intimate relationship between the owner and the text. Pen in hand, readers might communicate their feelings and thoughts about the author's words directly in the margins. The book was theirs to do with as they willed; they could make it work for them in any way they saw fit.

This conversation of personal preferences and connections should be honored when we're reading literature with students. These preferences and connections are the means for initiating democratic dialogue. One way of doing this is to grant authority to each individual's reading history. The tension that de Tocqueville identified between individual agency and dependency on public opinion is often evident in a reader's hesitancy to hold any views about a book until everything's been checked out with the critics, those cultural watchdogs in the business of informing us about what we should be thinking and feeling. Teachers of literature help break the tyranny of such a reliance on outside authority when they sanction the natural multiplicity of responses and interpretations that make up our social talk about literature. Recognizing that they bring distinct reading histories to a text can affirm for young readers the pleasures of reading. This is not just a matter of anchoring authority inside. Reading cannot be a social act if readers don't know or express their responses in conversation with others.

"You can say what you like about *Animal Farm,*" Glenda said, interrupting Tara, "but for me it was just a silly book."[1] She'd been listening patiently to Tara, all the while continuing to shake her head slowly, but now she boiled over. "Why read about all those animals? Tara, I know you really liked it, I know you saw all those symbols in it. Me, I couldn't make a thing out of it, I just couldn't get interested. So PLEASE stop trying to convince me." Then the girls both laughed. "Well," said Tara, "sometimes we agree on books and then sometimes we're miles apart. No, I'm not going to give up on you, especially when a book's as terrific as this one. But, okay, let's call it a day." And the conversation drifted to other things.

Glenda and Tara are good friends despite their frequent disagreements about their reading experiences. In coming to terms with their differences, they have learned to appreciate each other's individuality. Tara doesn't want to give up on Glenda; in some way their rift is unsettling: "Why can't she see what I see?"—each wonders about the other. Certainly, it would be more convenient if their tastes were neatly aligned. There would be no disagreements and each would feel confirmed in her stance toward experience. It is easier to seek out and move in circles of similarity and agreement rather than have to tolerate disparities in response and interpretation. Such a course, however, leads to our impoverishment as readers.

Once the iron clad conformity of the right response and attitude in the literature classroom is broken, a stimulating plurality of taste and enjoyment emerges. Asking students to track and share what they really do and prefer as readers is an important way of broadening the conversation, although we must be willing to entertain perspectives at odds with the formal curriculum. Here, for instance, is the voice of a student who is just finishing high school:

> Now for a confession—from the age of 13, I started to neglect my regular private reading. I much preferred to read non-fictional material, so although I read very few novels, I read many newspapers, magazines and non-fictional books. . . . My main problem these days is a lack of time for reading novels, and if I am brutally honest, an unwillingness to become absorbed in a world that is not reality. However, as *To Kill a Mockingbird* proved, there are a few books capable of winning me over again. (personal communication)

Another student also shows a keen awareness of the gap between what she feels and what she believes she should be feeling, when she confesses her pleasure at reading "trashy books":

> At this I hear all literary type people gasping with horror. These authors' books, in particular, Jackie Collins', are seen by many as being all the same—trashy, cheap and not worth the paper they are written on. Their critics accuse them of writing for the uncultured masses, regularly turning out novels that they know will sell well, but which have no value as literature. . . .
>
> I, and I know many other people, feel very guilty at reading this "rubbish" because of what the so-called experts say. I feel that as an English literature student I should spend all my free time reading "real" books—heavy, thick, dusty hardbacks that are written by a Russian, or at the very least, a French author.
>
> I hate myself for thinking like this and falling victim to the views of the pompous critics, but I can't help it. I know I should have the courage of my convictions and read what I like by who I like, but I still feel guilty. When I start to think about it, I am not even sure if these books are what I really like reading, sometimes I wonder if I read them because they are seen as books that I shouldn't be reading. When I was very young my books were always chosen for me. (personal communication)

In these two instances, and in countless others that disrupt the "proper" decorum of reading, exists an exciting conversation that the teacher might join. This is especially true when teachers share their own rich and varied reading patterns.

As the second student intimates, the problem is often more about *imposition* and *subordination,* than it is about any given title or selection. Yet, in numerous instances, teachers fear that students, if they are given free rein, will avoid the "classics" and thus lose an opportunity to become critical readers. What seems to be the case, however, is that once legitimate participation in choosing books is denied, there is a natural inclination to opt out of the process altogether—that is, read *nothing.* On the other hand, to get past the rigid order of any "approved" book list allows reading possibilities and connections to explode in wonderful profusion. The only admission that teachers must be willing to make at this point is that they'll never be able to keep up with all the titles. Hopefully, this inadequacy will not be an excuse for restricting any student's reading range or perspective. An adult shows interest in student reading, not by imposing books, but by being attentive to the various dialogues they are interested in pursuing about the reading experiences *they* have initiated among themselves.

Democratically Sharing Our Cultural Knowledge

As textual information in our culture (books, music, art, film) continues to explode exponentially, no one, under the press of normal circumstances, can ever hope to stay abreast in order to command all the possible intertextual references needed for a complete response and interpretation. Adding other areas of knowledge—including biography, history, and science—the experience of trying to exhaust all literary reference for a complete reading is truly overwhelming. This shouldn't imply that we give up in frustration or ignorance. Instead, remembering these humbling realities helps me be more sympathetic to student readers. I can see how they often feel unable to join the reading conversation, because they believe they know too little. First, they don't have to recognize or understand everything—nobody ever does. But, second, they need to avoid debilitating comparisons with those who more readily burst forth with interpretive commentary. Unfortunately, students spend more time learning what they can't do as readers, rather than simply getting on with the task of revealing what's on their minds in concert with others.

Popular culture texts such as Billy Joel's hit single, "We Didn't Start the Fire"—with it's refrain about the world always burning in controversy—serve to put the whole information game in its proper perspective. With verses that contain an endless list of names and events from the past—Joseph Stalin, Hemingway, the cola wars—this song reverberates more intensely as one recognizes more items. Paralleling Don McLean's "American Pie," or Alan Ginsberg's poems such as "America," Joel's lyrics acknowledge that interpretations depend on people sharing a heritage and not displaying total amnesia of the past.

But references demand a kind of communal layering; they're not just correct answers on some multiple-choice exam. The teacher's credibility in working with students on such a lyric grows out of her ability to create a shared pool of knowledge, drawing as equally on the students' resources as on her own. Each person expresses some bafflement; each can make some connections. With a democratic sense of the continuing information explosion and overload, we are able to defuse any elitist aspects of cultural knowledge and instead find ourselves all contributing items to E. D. Hirsch's list of what every American should know (see Hirsch, 1987). This means students become aware of what bits of information serve as markers for membership in what groups—a quite different matter than hierarchically legislating what is to count as "common" knowledge.

Attacks on cultural pluralism and the democratization of the canon show a deep disdain for the untutored. Those attempting to maintain their stranglehold of prejudice that derives from the "great books" argue that substitution or expansion will lead to a natural diminution of quality and standards. Fearing difference and encouraging feelings of nostalgia in order to mask their own privileged position as interpreters of these "sacred" texts, canon defenders create a fiction of coherence that, they would have us believe, must be maintained at all costs. There is a deep irony in trying to replace the broad spirit of Western inquiry with authoritarian readings of specific cultural artifacts. The quest for liberty—for freedom of thought and exploration—and the scientific method are, in fact, what created the very conditions that allowed all kinds of previously silenced groups and perspectives to eventually make their claims on our attention.

The raucous clamor to be recognized is certainly disconcerting when it seems to be dislodging a given set of texts and interpretations already securely in place. But this is precisely what fulfills the cumulative promise of our Western thought and intellectual tradition. Surely a restless critical spirit is what should animate our academic tradition. In addition to closing down access, there is a further danger when any group claims the higher ground and attempts to restrict dialogue. Ironically, they end up offering exactly the wrong model for multicultural advocates. Without dialogue, those who hold a minority viewpoint and preach a culture of exclusion risk isolating themselves from the mainstream. Indeed, in Balkan fashion, they feel self-righteously justified in not entering the larger cultural conversation. Such splintering and segregation voids negotiation and thereby lowers every reader's horizons.

Obviously, a society is constituted on the basis of some commonality in order that citizens are able to speak with one another. Given a deliberate effort, what students read in the curriculum will be widely representative and varied, and not narrowly directed toward compartmentalized perspectives. This representativeness, however, can never be taken for granted, but must be consciously cultivated. Researchers have well documented a *selective tradition,* in which teachers choose books for use in the literature curriculum that reflect their own circumscribed worlds and biases (see Luke et al, 1986; also Jipson and Paley, 1991). Still, the burden of community does not fall on what specific texts we read together. No, the burden falls on the ways we read together.

Democracy relies on a tacit faith in fairness and a willingness to see that decisions serve more than the immediate self-interest of specially advantaged citizens. But despite this important principle of equality and fair play, the force of accumulated social tradition and the hidden exercise of power keep verticality unexamined and securely in place. Central to this verticality is the deeply ingrained belief that lies behind the refrain, The people are not to be fully trusted. This moral and intellectual heritage needs to be uncovered for what it is, if we are to change those educational practices that run counter to democratic principles. For until we free ourselves from unconsciously acting in a paternalistic manner toward all those who have not yet reached our level of attainment, we can never hope to see the other from his or her perspective.

Often our social and occupational positions are maintained through routines that insist on the dependency of clients. We seem invested in retaining others in some state of immaturity. I can say I want students to be independent, but then quickly turn around and hold them back because they have not yet adequately met some standard. What's really at issue here is my lack of faith in their ability to know what's good for them. Even while I may think everyone's entitled to equal rights and opportunities, any deviation from *my* view of things can suddenly appear as provoking disorder— which is really threatening *my* order, *my* authority. From here it is

only a small leap to seeing difference and change as bad and therefore wanting to keep all others in their place.

Privilege and distrust work hand in hand. Thus the real message
contained in any plea that would return the curriculum to the "good
old days" is that access should be limited. People are not to be trusted with their own intelligence, nor with their own welfare or language. In contrast, open engagement with texts encourages us to
take seriously perspectives alien from our own. And it is this experience that keeps us from being locked in the present and concluding that history and human consciousness are inevitably on a
downward spiral. But to see outside, we must also be looking inside
to understand our own perceptions.

Tapping Our Reading Histories

The literature lesson, as I see it, is very much about each student's
evolving answer to the ongoing saga of, What kind of reader am I?
This means, however, that we have to act so as to include every last
student as part of this inquiry. Even the reluctant need to have their
voices heard. Here, for instance, are the views of fourteen-year-old
Eric,[2] who would prefer never to be sitting in a literature class. I
have interspersed his written words with what I imagine a teacher
might be thinking in response, impressions a teacher might draw on
in talking with Eric.

Eric: I'm the sort of person who does'nt like to read.[*sic*]

Teacher: *So that's a big divide: those who like to read, those who don't. I
wonder if that's just a natural inclination or a habit or a taste one develops
or is prevented from developing?*

Eric: But if I ever do have to read I read a book about mystery and sus-
pense or a comedy.

Teacher: *There's something about that rush-to-turn-the-page quality of a
book. Sometimes I leave a book unfinished because I don't really care
about what's going to happen next to the characters. Eric, what is it about
a story that keeps you involved?*

Eric: The places I have red a book is in bed or in the sitting room when
there nothing on T.V. The worst place to read I think is in the kitchen on
the loo or where there's people about. I like to sit in complete silence.[*sic*]

Teacher: *Sometimes I can read with music going, but I'd mostly agree with
you about the silence. I seem to read better in the evening. Does time of day
make a difference for you? Can you read at all in school? I know I find it
hard to concentrate when lots of other things are on my mind.*

Eric: I learnt to read when I was about 4. My mum ran an playgroup and she used to help me to read. I started on basics like cards with small words on.[*sic*]

Teacher: *Do you remember having any fun doing this? Was it hard? What story writing did you do then? Did the other kids look forward to reading?*

Eric: Then when I was at school we had a set of about 10 books ranging from hard to easy.

Teacher: *What were they like? I wonder if what was hard and what was easy varied from child to child. And if that was the case, it would be interesting to know if you got to choose some of your own books during this time. Did anyone ever use a library?*

Eric: At night my mum used to read to me. Sometimes night time stories or comic books.

Teacher: *I remember especially being read Grimm's fairy tales when I was sick. Do you still like listening to stories being read out loud?*

Eric: I prefor watching T.V. more and when I do I like any sort of thriller or comedy.

Teacher: *So you like the same kind of stories, whether in books or on T.V. I like it when at first no one will believe the victim and then gradually the evidence becomes overwhelming and the authorities are forced to change their minds—hopefully before it's too late!*

By staying in touch with what the reader is telling us, rather than judging or feeling ourselves superior, the authority of our position as teachers can be used to enforce the idea that readers are entitled to their own likes and dislikes. This is the beginning point of democratic discussions of literature.

Our reading histories also extend to detailed accounts of how our feelings and understandings evolve while we're reading individual works. If developing readers learn to focus on what happens when *they* read, then, as Donald Fry suggests, "they will grow into an awareness of themselves reading, which is another way of coming to understand how they learn, how they live, how they are" (Fry, p. 107). This ongoing self-reflection, done in the midst of an accepting environment, breeds confidence in one's abilities because it sees reading as a self-correcting process. But again, this kind of reflection is a social phenomenon: if we don't share our predictions and hunches with others, we have no way of tapping into the larger pool of resources that we need to confirm and stretch the verisimilitude of our own readings.

Many literature teachers now encourage their students to keep reading logs to chart their emerging engagement with what they are reading. This allows one's reading, especially of novels, to be anchored in time. While sometimes we have the luxury to read a book straight through, more often it's the case that we move slowly through a story as it unfolds. This might mean that perhaps our mood will not always be the same as we come to read different sections of a book, or perhaps we'll not remember every detail over time. Once a novel is finished, however, and all that remains is a sense of global awareness, we easily forget the accumulating energy that was being invested as we moved through the pages sequentially. Keeping a record dramatically demonstrates the changes of direction our readings often take and therefore can make us more sensitive to and tolerant of the vagaries of other readers. Showing students that they have a reading process and history worth considering certainly helps to give them an added sense of power and participation. Even younger, less-sophisticated students will eagerly join a common inquiry in this way.

Recently, in England, I was talking over these ideas with some middle school students and their teacher. Afterward, one of the girls, Rosa, presented me with a log she had kept for 35 days while she was making her way through *Goodnight Mister Tom* by Michelle Magorian. Rosa, who had recently immigrated to England, begins her twenty-one-page saga by copying the blurb on the dust jacket about how Willie Beech, a deprived boy from London, who is sent to the country just before the outbreak of World War II, flourishes under the care of an elderly pensioner—but soon his happiness is deflated when he's called back home by his mother. Then Rosa continues, setting down how she feels oriented to the book before actually beginning her reading. This serves as a baseline for a series of changes that will subsequently take place:

> I only chose this book, 'cause Sarah suggested it to me. The title seemed boring to me. . . . The front isn't really that thrilling, it looks like a book that goes for ever and never comes to the interesting parts. I read the hype (or whatever, you know, the thingy). It sounded pretty good, especially the part where it says, "Knows just how to grab the emotions." I'm that sort, you see, cries at nearly everything sissy!
>
> There's absolutely no connection between me and the old fogey on the front. Seriously, there isn't.
>
> I guess I expect to find my self crying when I'm finished with it. Sarah reckon's it's really sad. In this kind of book I think I'll expect really "big" words, you know like, "ostentatious" (I bet I've spelt that wrong, eh?) bye.[3]

Rosa's entries are generally addressed directly to her teacher, who establishes an accepting and attentive partnership with her in the course of her reading. In the margins, he banters back and forth supportively. In response to her spelling anxiety, for example, he writes, "No—it's right. Miracles!" Rosa can speak freely for she knows she'll get a caring and honest reaction back. Thus, well into the second chapter of the novel, Rosa comments, "I like the way Michelle has used Tom's accent. If I wrote something like that it'll probably get corrected into proper English even though it's in an accent (you dig??)." To which her teacher replies, "If it's an accent, I wouldn't correct it & no—I don't like gardening." Or when Rosa copies out a line that's confused her in the novel, "He added some *coke* to the fire," (her italics) and writes, "Weird, ha? I wouldn't chuck my can of coke in the fire!!!? Coke, what's it mean?" again her teacher comes back humorously with, "Wally—It's a form of coal."

Throughout these beginning chapters, Rosa continues looking for a place to enter and connect with the lives presented in the novel. "Even at the beginning of the book the emotions are coming on strong. . . . So far there's no connections between me & the book, (don't really expect there to be)." She gives her ongoing impressions, even as she searches for expressions that she can't quite manage:

> I've just finished reading the 2nd chapter, & I can already see the relationship between Willie and Tom is getting stronger, and more . . . (you know what the word is (?) I can't remember, never mind (?!)) Yes, well, anyway, I'm going to carry on reading now!

Several pages later in her log, Rosa quotes another line, "The sheets were drenched in urine," and adds a comment that is surprisingly close to self: "(HO, HO!!) Fancy that, Willie wet his bed! Actually to be honest, that's the only connection between the book & me so far! (HA, HA!)." Throughout, Rosa writes in a colloquial style that keeps her close to her personal judgments of what she understands to be going on in the novel: "The characters are pretty naf, ain't they?, I mean personality ways. But the author has obviously thought very carefully about the kind of characters she wanted, & I think that the author has succeeded." Still, through most of her log she remains very much on the fence, not sure that this story will ever deliver for her: "I knew it was gonna be one of those books that never comes to the interesting part."

Much of Rosa's log is, of course, taken up with plot summaries of the story. This kind of retelling repetition helps Rosa draw the story inside herself, making it more her own. Yet even these summaries are peppered with her valuative reactions and reveal her as an active, responding reader:

> Will was holding the baby in his arms, he had bruises all over the place. (Surprise "bloomin" Surprise!?). Will has been taken to hospital. Tom, Sammey & the Warden went along too! The baby was dead, they haven't told Will yet. That was so sad when Will went

home (but I didn't cry!) It wasn't dramatic enough for me to cry, but was very emotional.

When at last Rosa comes to the end of the novel, she finds she's surprised even herself: "Finis! I didn't think I was going to cry! I actually cried! When they announced Zach's death, my heart missed a beat, there was a lump in my throat and the 'bloomin' tears trickled down my cheek!" Here was a character that really moved her and cemented her relationship to the story: "It was as though Zach was the only character that was alive. He was the one I could actually feel his presence in my mind. I was crying for such a long time I just couldn't believe it. Zach reminds me of someone, but I can't remember who."

Finally, in her concluding remarks that complete this reading cycle, Rosa begins with some reflections on herself as reader:

> As a reader, I've learned that I'm not a good reader. I'll be reading something & then suddenly I'll think who the hell is this?! My concentration seems to drift away when I'm reading.

Next, she sizes up the whole story and offers a word of advice to the author, whom she continues to address unabashedly by her first name:

> The book had a very nice slow beginning, at the end I didn't want the book to end.
>
> I reckon that Michelle has her own "unique" kind of way of writing a novel. I like her style, it's definitely different to any other books I've read.
>
> If Michelle were to re-write this book I'd tell her to cut the crap about Will meeting new people short & make the bit with his friends, getting along really well, longer. She should write about what they do as a "team," what adventures they want to do & all that.

Her closing words are more than ample testimony of how her 35-day persistence in the reading of this novel has paid off: "My opinions of the book have definitely changed. I use to think this book was the same & boring as any other book. But now I think it's really good." In her very hands, Rosa now owns a permanent record of dialogue with her teacher, one that illustrates the dynamic interplay between the personal and the social that constitutes her reading. By faithfully writing in her log, Rosa has discovered that she counts as a reader.

As we look more deeply into readers' responses, their ongoing attempts to make sense of some aesthetic stimulus, we see in what flux they exist. Responses, in other words, are very much temporally determined. They change cumulatively through time. As Rosa's log entries illustrate, one's final response to a story does not capture all the nuances of the accruing record of the journey. Indeed, taking the final response in isolation, we might conclude that reading *in time* is a fairly straightforward affair. Yet any close inspection of actual readers, such as Rosa, shows that there is finally no set pattern. In fact, the strange and unpredictable twists and turns of response are frequently the rule, not the exception—which I am constantly reminded whenever I track my own readings in time.

Admitting Our Reading Mishaps

One such response shift startled me while I was watching the movie *Lorenzo's Oil* (1992), starring Susan Sarandon and Nick Nolte. For some reason, it didn't register with me that this film was a docudrama. Apparently my eavesdropping on TV commercials for the movie had been most inattentive. Further, I don't believe in quick and miraculous cures for unknown maladies; I share my wife's prejudice against what she labels the "illness of the week TV movie." All this left me with a set of formulaic expectations as the screen lit up before me. I thought this was going to be a movie about a family reaching to all lengths in order to cure a ghastly ill child, and at the last minute they would find some magical cure and the child would climb out of bed and resume a normal life.

Given this predisposition, it took me awhile to piece together what I was seeing on the screen. Several times during the movie, the camera glances over an object, a knife with an elaborately carved handle, and so I was waiting for this knife from East Africa to be the key to the plot. I read it as anticipating some witch doctor, who would then save the boy in the nick of time with a magic spell or potion. On the other hand, even as I tried to suspend my disbelief that miracles can happen, I found myself wishing that this suffering, emaciated child might just be allowed to die in peace.

Then slowly it dawned on me that the director was making a special effort to offer verisimilitude for the parents' quest for a scientifically valid treatment for this rare disease, adrenoleukodystrophy. For instance, the father spends countless hours at a medical research library delving into the secrets of fatty acids and organic chemistry. Models of the brain and the central nervous system appear, and I'm confronted with schematic diagrams of myelin, which I associate with myelopathy—a disease that killed my own father.

This began to seem like a real malady. Did the olive oil, which the parents begin giving Lorenzo at the end of the movie, actually hold some recuperative power?

Finally, the actual chronology of scenes is emphasized. For example, it's March 14, 1985, six months after the first diagnosis, and time is marching on. Nor does any magic spell or potion appear, despite the family's recruitment of a caring African from the village where the family had previously lived. At that time, this man had befriended Lorenzo and now, most sympathetically, he comes to serve as part of the care procedure. Despite this gradual reorientation away from my original response expectations, it shocked me how far off the mark my predictive map had been. The movie had, in fact, been based on the story of a real family's controversial struggle against an entrenched medical bureaucracy.

As my interpretation took a new shape, it was possible to reread the pattern of symbolism in the movie. No longer was it necessary to see the knife as a symbol of alchemy or magic; now it appeared as a sign of unity and continuity with the African. After making the long journey to a strange culture, he creates a special bond with the sick boy, who is seemingly locked forever outside the bounds of human communication. The African senses a living connection beyond human words and so strengthens the parents' resolve not to give up on their son's valiant effort to stay in touch, however tenuously, with the world of the living.

In sharing with my students how I felt thrown off in my viewing of *Lorenzo's Oil,* I try to demonstrate the many routes we end up taking to capture a work for ourselves. What is interesting about our initial reading of any text is that we can never quite relive the mystery and excitement of coming upon the puzzle of the words and the situations for the first time. By keeping our reading temporally located, we help defeat the notion of closure and "correct" interpretations. Seeing variety in the readings of others authorizes it to exist in ourselves. Cultivating such reflection in the reading process allows us to be expansive in our view of what can take place in the literature classroom.

The democratic process of reading literature exists to widen the circle of readers of all ages. It accepts their experience, whatever it's been, and links it into new combinations of significance. Each reading history bears testimony to the inquiring social nature of our minds, if curiosity has not already been leeched from them. Frederic J. Oates, for instance, began auditing college courses at age seventy, after spending forty years in the tool and die business. The father of Joyce Carol Oates, he tells, in "New Kid on Campus," of the particular reading pleasures that came about in classes where he was taken seriously as reader. To begin with, he inherited his love of poetry from his mother, "who always had collections of her favorite poems about the house" (Oates, p. 58). The fiction that he read in his early years "was the usual adventure stories, like *Tom Swift, The Rover Boys* and, a little later, *Gulliver's Travels, Tom Sawyer* and such." Yet he recognized even then that "there was something different about the two types of stories, something more than one of them being entertainment for children." He "wasn't to know the extent of the differences, however, for some years to come" (p. 58).

Although Oates had always been "an avid reader of fiction and poetry," by returning to school after all those years, and rejoining the conversation, he began to see the need to pause and probe his "reading in terms of its significance." In slowing down and reflecting on his reading process, he learned "to analyze, judge, look beneath the surface, question prejudices and easy assumptions." The point was to "see and hear and think in terms altogether different from those of daily life." This process of give and take carried out under the teacher's careful "prodding," made otherwise inaccessible books enjoyable for the first time:

> One that comes to mind is Faulkner's *The Sound and the Fury.*
> How many of us, I wonder, bogged down in the first section, and
> just got tired of what seemed gibberish? That story was given a
> fresh outlook after Benjy's "narrations" were brought into focus.
> For me, it became one of Faulkner's best. (p. 58)

Such broadly inclusive reading practices gradually gave Oates the confidence to see himself as an agent in his own literary education. His story about doing "something daring" in a class shows how the reading of literature expands when teachers feel free to move in unprepared directions:

> I came to English class early and, without my professor's knowl-
> edge, distributed copies of a poem he had written, which I had
> seen in a local publication. The poem titled "Braille," was about
> people touching the names of the dead on the Vietnam War memo-
> rial in Washington, D.C. We got the professor to talk about the
> poem, and it led to one of our most fascinating discussions and an
> excellent impromptu reading. We experienced "poetry in motion,"
> and I doubt any of us will forget it. (p. 58)

Oates' reading history disconfirms any elitist visions of who is able to read what. Because the instruction democratically invited his participation, Oates surprised himself with a burst of energy and self-recognition, just as Rosa had done. By staying in touch with his own responses as a reader, Oates could begin to appreciate the pressing human dimension of the literary conversation. How might we as teachers ensure that this happens for all our students, whatever their age or ability?

Notes

1. This conversation is printed with the permission of its participants.
2. This student's views are reprinted with his permission.
3. Selections from this student's journal are printed with her permission.

Chapter Fifteen

Invitations and Possibilities

Toward the end of *My Country School Diary,* the vital account of her democratic teaching experience in a one-room schoolhouse, Miss Julia Weber offers this testimony:

> I have found that I can learn to do things I never did before. I, too, can meet life creatively and help to make it a better place for me and my fellow men. It is the most wonderful, most encouraging and hopeful feeling one can have! I think I can understand a little better why Walt Whitman always wanted to sing about everything. (Gordon, p. 197)

In intelligently progressive ways, Weber placed the creative inquiry of her students within the boundaries of community relationships. While the task of learning engaged individuals in their specificity, its orientation repeatedly emphasized the social perspective that prepares citizens to live in a democracy. Weber was not ambivalent or apologetic about this purpose. She stood firmly for an education that sensitively acknowledged and negotiated the differences among people. The patterns of her lessons, the configurations of her classroom, tell a story of teacher and students living within the care and respect of relationship.

The reason Weber speaks with such joy and affirmation is that she deeply understood how confidence serves as bulwark for competence. Every student desires attention, but this attention is really a call for being taken seriously, for being seen as a distinct person by the teacher. In straightforward, open conversation with students, which incorporated *their* responses, Weber gave to each student her full concentration. What she discovered in making this talk reciprocal, in being a good listener, was that students came to feel included in a joint endeavor. Because their words counted, the students learned to develop confidence in conversation. Through the give and take of conversation about what mattered crucially in their lives, the students came to participate in the community in which they lived, discovering capacities and possibilities that otherwise, had they remained in silence, they would never have known.

What Weber accomplished as a teacher stemmed directly from her commitment to democratic relationships. The secret entailed cultivating in her students the confidence to both speak out and to listen. In her school, Weber enacted the vital habits of democracy that John Dewey had outlined: following an argument, grasping the other's point of view, expanding mutual understanding, and discussing alternative objectives that might be pursued. "Strange as it may seem to an era governed by mass-market politics," William Greider tells us, "democracy begins in human conversation" (Greider, p. 411). Through talk, ordinary people "engage themselves with their surrounding reality" and, thus, might "question the conflict between what they are told and what they see and experience" (p. 410). For, as Greider concludes, "the simplest, least threatening investment any citizen may make in democratic renewal is to begin talking with other people about these questions, as though the answers matter to them" (p. 411). Such conversations of inquiry in a democracy acknowledge the fact that people are willing to talk through their "unalterable" beliefs and opinions.

Uncertainty and Tolerance

Literary works have the power to unsettle readers. In democratic fashion, they invite interpretation, change, and innovation—that is when readers actively converse with texts, not just passively receive them. Poetry, in other words, confirms, even while it disconfirms, or at least extends, our perceptions and conceptions of the world. We are bound together as we enact and share the irony of our repeated differences and contradictions. Texts exist in terms of our social conversation with them. This means that we are able to learn from them precisely because they are different from us and therefore provoke our sense of alternate beliefs in the world. Only by according the "difference" of the text its due can we reach outside our own confining beliefs and prejudices and encounter other points of view.

A democracy of readers and readings draws on the imagination, which might be defined as our ability to construct alternatives worlds of human experience. Once there is room in our consciousness for more than one conception of human motives and actions, we've begun to constitute space for the *other*. The humanities' plea for *tolerance*—perhaps the central invention of Western thought—emphasizes how hard it is to live with difference and how much more comfortable we feel with the kind of straight thinking that would keep difference safely contained. How frightening a democratic, poststructuralist sensibility must appear to persons who drive down the highway sporting, with no hint of irony, bumper stickers that proclaim, "God said it/ I believe it/ And that's the end of it." People who yearn for the homogeneity of a completely common culture, who deeply need a devil to hate, cling to cultural absolutes that often make it hard for them to respect, in the spirit of democracy, the dignity of the other person.

When one side is tied firmly to all-encompassing beliefs and the other side is tolerant, collective action is difficult. This is why "we must not," Isaiah Berlin emphasizes, "dramatize the incompatibility of values—there is a great deal of broad agreement among people in different societies over long stretches of time about what is right and wrong, good and evil."[1] The liberal position, which makes democracy possible, grows out of a long-held Western tradition of attempting to live with uncertainty, of attempting to incorporate the doubt of the *other*. This tradition does lead to various forms of relativism by not insisting on absolute beliefs. Still, without its foundation of tolerance, all other competing values war themselves to death.

But advocating tolerance and understanding, we cannot ignore the corresponding urgency of active commitment—a tolerance for ambiguity need not be a cover for weakness or inaction. Indeed, politely and indiscriminately granting every right demanded by others can quickly lead to conflict, especially when the rights of the deeply prejudiced are not somehow held in check. This often occurs when the multicultural agenda is expressed as demands and divisions, rather than conversations. When the point of diversity is to issue ultimatums and promote isolated fragmentation, then the desire of democracy becomes subverted. Edward Rothstein, in fact, sees this movement in terms of entrapment:

> Multiculturalism has no use for the heritage of liberalism . . . or for the energies of modernism. It is, at bottom, folkish Romanticism gone bad. Its calls for equity derive not from recognized unity, but from enforced difference. It takes other cultures seriously only as representations of the merely particular. Multiculturalism fails to see the Other within us, or us within the Other. As a result, it undoes the very notion of Western culture. (Rothstein, pp. 33–34)

This suggests that the debate about pluralism must *not* center on the specific artifacts of a culture; rather, it should encourage broad cultural conversations as part of each citizen's experience. Conflicting loyalties, and the deep passions that lie behind them, may, of course, obstruct social encounters, but these loyalties need to be placed in some larger context committed to democratic relationships.

The democratic process of reading as a *social activity* cannot overcome the potential impasse between tolerance and belief, but it can keep us focused on the difference between genuine claims to fairness and intolerant fundamentalist doctrines associated with transcendental belief systems. Liberal tolerance itself has to be militant, or dominance and submission will come to characterize our public relationships. We must be clear just how fragile our democratic ideas and institutions are. When certainty is the primary value, it is natural for each person to want their viewpoint to triumph. Yet such a triumph can only happen when other viewpoints—and thus uncertainty—are completely silenced. When he talked about the deterioration of the mind that occurs under a "ban placed on all inquiry which does not end in the orthodox conclusions," John Stuart Mill succinctly located the real tragedy of an intolerant contemporary society: "The greatest harm done is to those who are not heretics, and whose whole mental development is cramped, and their reason cowed, by the fear of heresy" (Mill, p. 39).

It has never been easy protecting the rights of unpopular minorities, though a starting point continues to be the reading responses that might occur in a literature class. Reading literature with students is an opportunity for using the uncertainty of response and interpretation to democracy's advantage. Because a reader's responses and interpretations are not unalterable, not infallible, he or she might move toward realizing alternatives. Selves potentially proliferate. To be locked into any one interpretation, no matter how fitting for the moment, is to surrender the genius of our mental capacities—our ability to celebrate simultaneously *difference* and *similarity*, even in the face of socializing traditions that seek to predetermine each stage of our response. In this sense, reading literature can be the grandest, if most frustrating, of curriculum endeavors precisely because it can continue to entertain the riches of contradiction without destroying itself.

Acknowledging the rightful claim of each reader's uniqueness begins the practice of democracy, which then includes sharing responses across persons and tentatively exploring mutual understandings—shifting between what separates and what ties together. We may begin as other, as stranger, but the goal is to join a conversation and reach points of contact rather than conform to the certainties of answers already provided. The teaching/learning task is to place and negotiate in some safe, middle zone the meanings evoked during the reading of literature. Culture, age, experience, class, gender—they all provide opportunities to interweave positions of both difference and similarity. Without tolerance—without any understanding of the role each reader's prior script plays in the process of reading—it is difficult to experiment with the kind of talk required to ensure that reading proceeds as a social activity.

Entertaining ambiguity and complexity nudges the reader into a space of uncertainty, which in turn is rendered safe because it is a shared space. To read in solitary fashion is to miss the multiplicity of possible responses and interpretations others might contribute. In our social capacity as reader, we discover that often our interpretations are actually invented to stay in conversation with others. In responding to texts we are amazed to find the sociality of our individuality.

One of de Tocqueville's concerns was that "in modern society, everything threatens to become so much alike, that the peculiar characteristics of each individual will soon be entirely lost in the general aspect of the world" (de Tocqueville, p. 326). He also noted that in a democracy, "literature will not easily be subjected to strict rules, and it is impossible that any such rules should ever be permanent" (p. 161). By encouraging readers to live with uncertainty, democratic reading uses literature as a way of keeping each individual reader in sight. Because its rules resist permanence, the "unfinished" text keeps alive the hope that democracy, in giving birth to the individual, will not also preside over her death.

Alive in Each Other

In a democracy, the text stands poised among competing points of view. Returning to it again and again is our fundamental way of adjudicating disagreements and dissension. Thus, to consider reading—and writing—as a transactional social act is to recognize *reading* as a deliberately constructed stance, one that grows out of a commitment to democratic social arrangements. Exchanging and modifying reading responses through discussion with others is no more natural than keeping everything locked up within us.

So what advantages result from discouraging isolated, competitive reading? Certainly, many will claim that they do not consider, nor have ever encountered, reading as a social act; but this is the result of hierarchical socialization, something many students experience as alienating. An NYU graduate student, born and educated in India, gives this account of how a cultural system can rigidly constrain any open and free exchange:

> Sharing one's writing or showing it to someone other than the instructor, is a concept which is practically non-existent in the Indian education system. Nobody even thinks of sharing his/her writing with his/her peers, for the purpose of getting feedback. If at all papers are shared, as they sometimes are amongst friends, it is not with the intention of seeking a response to help revise the paper, but simply to glean the contents of it and not offer anything more than a cursory remark or two. It took me a while to get used to the idea of showing my writing to my peers, but now that I am more comfortable with it, I find it to be an immense help in revising my papers. Also, It has somewhat dispelled the notion of writing as a totally private activity. (personal communication)

Democracy, by its very nature, is in a struggle with alternate ways of organizing both knowledge and people. We cannot escape the consequences of the relationships we establish, if we hope to widen avenues of access.

The social relationships within which we share our readings of literature inevitably inform our practices as teachers. Wanting these relationships to be democratic constitutes a specific commitment to shaping conversational encounters in the classroom. If we are to live up to democracy's promise to encourage the full development of all individuals in the group, then, in the literature class at least, we begin by ensuring that all students have the right to their own reading responses as part of a continuing social conversation. What matters most about the reading of literature in a democracy is not *what* the text actually means, but *how*, together, we go about making it mean whatever it does. Inadequate meanings will be winnowed out when each of us has our say in relation to the other.

Literary response need not search for the closure of a final personal meaning. What is wanted is collaborative negotiation so we can share and learn from each other's interpretations. Yet negotiation fares badly when the precise preferences of the parties are fixed in advance. In reading texts socially, readers shift among many responses in order to keep the process open. Thus, interpretations become more satisfying, because they are both anchored in and developed beyond our original response positions.

Within the teacher-student reading relationship we might begin to redistribute power more equitably. This would encourage students to take a second look at what is happening in the classroom. Exploring issues of control, students might become aware of the ideological constraints that will determine their motives and actions when their turn comes to hold power over others. When the teacher explicitly builds into the curriculum collaborative strategies of negotiation, students learn to manage the crisis of authority, especially when it is raised in matters of textual interpretation. Because texts and assignments are partially indeterminant, and therefore problematic in the sense that they exist as social constructions, the teacher's real authority derives from preventing readings from becoming reified. Students, mostly, do not like living in this state of uncertainty, so they demand a hierarchical system, one in which they can unquestioningly fit. This, however, blocks the route to responsibility. With someone else setting the lessons, students remain dependent. They fail to gain the autonomy they need to blossom as citizens in a democracy.

Teachers and students come confidently to each new poem whon thoir provious oxporioncoo with pooms havc bccn affirming. This happens when each of us is allowed to trust and share the meanings we have found in the words we've been reading. The sense of security required for this trust to occur is fundamental to democratic living. A social approach to the reading of literature invites us all to honor multiple perspectives. We value ambiguity and indeterminacy, because it allows us to combine our unique individuality with our profound desire for correspondence. In the reading matrix, we establish meanings that link us to other readers also developing their interpretations. Democracy presupposes that an individual's freedom and possibilities are best expanded when there is a creative balance between self and group. This happens through imaginative recognitions of one another.

When I first began as a teacher of literature I believed I *alone* was responsible for supplying the interpretations in the classroom. I felt I could stand apart from the mess of democratic negotiation and just float safely in realms of abstraction—distant from the conundrums of difference. But, eventually, I awoke and found I was missing the affirming pleasures of vulnerability and intimacy within the classroom conversation. No longer blind to the reciprocal quality of reading encounters, I began to invite students to share in their enactment. It took the readings of others to balance the frustrations with the satisfactions of democratic relationships. "So I said yes. Now we are alive in each other."

Note

1. As quoted by Michael Ignatieff. 29 April 1991. "The Ends of Empathy." *New Republic* 204(17): 34.

Works Cited

Auspitz, Josiah Lee. 1991. "Michael Oakeshott: 1901–1990." *American Scholar* 60(3): 351–70.

Barthes, Roland. 1986. *The Responsibility of Forms: Critical Essays on Music, Art, and Representation*. Oxford: Basil Blackwell.

Baylor, Byrd and Peter Parhall. 1978. *The Other Way to Listen*. New York: Chas. Scribner's.

Bloom, Harold. 1973. *The Anxiety of Influence*. New York: Oxford University Press.

Britton, James. 1982. "Shaping at the Point of Utterance." In: Gordon M. Pradl, ed. *Prospect & Retrospect: Selected Essays of James Britton*. Montclair, NJ: Boynton-Cook, 139–45.

Broughton, Esther and Janine Rider. 1991. "Writing about Literature with Large-Group Collaboration: The We-Search Paper." *English Leadership Quarterly* 13(3): 7–9.

Brown, Lyn Mikel and Carol Gilligan. 1992. *Meeting at the Crossroads: Woman's Psychology and Girl's Development*. Cambridge, MA: Harvard University Press.

Bruner, Jerome. 1990. *Acts of Meaning*. Cambridge, MA: Harvard University Press.

Burnheim, John. 1985. *Is Democracy Possible?* Berkeley, CA: University of California Press.

Canterford, Barbara. 1991. "The 'New' Teacher: Participant and Facilitator." *Language Arts* 68(4): 286–91.

Cherryholmes, Cleo H. 1988. *Power and Criticism: Poststructural Investigations in Education*. New York: Teachers College Press.

Christian-Smith, Linda K. 1990. *Becoming a Woman through Romance*. New York: Routledge.

Davies, Robertson. 1993. "A Reading Lesson." *Wilson Quarterly* 17(2): 99–105.

de Tocqueville, Alexis. 1964. *Democracy in America*. Andrew Hacker, ed. New York: Washington Square Press.

Dewey, John. 1916/1966. *Democracy and Education*. New York: Free Press.

Dewey, John. 1922. *Human Nature and Conduct*. New York: Henry Holt and Co.

Dewey, John. 1960. *The Quest for Certainty: A Study of the Relation of Knowledge and Action*. New York: G. P. Putnam's Sons (Capricorn Books).

Dewey, John. 1934/1980. *Art and Experience*. New York: Perigee Books.

Dewey, John and Arthur F. Bentley. 1949. *Knowing and the Known*. Boston: Beacon Press.

Dias, Patrick. 1987. *Making Sense of Poetry: Patterns in the Process*. Ottawa: Canadian Council of Teachers of English.

Donaldson, Margaret. 1992. *Human Minds*. New York: Allen Lane.

Durant, Will. 1927. *The Story of Philosophy*. New York: Simon & Schuster.

Ehrenreich, Barbara. 1989. *Fear of Falling: The Inner Life of the Middle Class*. New York: Pantheon Books.

Freedman, Audrey. July 12, 1989. "Those Costly 'Good Old Boys'." *New York Times*, section A, p. 23.

Fry, Donald. 1985. *Children Talk about Books: Seeing Themselves as Readers*. Milton Keynes, England: Open University Press.

Gere, Anne Ruggles, Colleen Fairbanks, Alan Howes, Laura Roop, and David Schaafsma. 1992. *Language and Reflection: An Integrated Approach to Teaching English*. New York: Macmillan.

Gilligan, Carol. 1982. *In a Different Voice*. Cambridge, MA: Harvard University Press.

Gordon, Julia Weber. 1946/1970. *My Country School Diary*. New York: Dell Publishing.

Greider, William. 1992. *Who Will Tell the People: The Betrayal of American Democracy*. New York: Simon & Schuster.

Hawthorne, Nathaniel. 1835/1964. "Young Goodman Brown." In: *Selected Tales and Sketches*. New York: Holt, Rinehart and Winston.

Hirsch, E. D. 1967. *Validity in Interpretation*. New Haven, CT: Yale University Press.

Hirsch, E. D. 1987. *Cultural Literacy: What Every American Needs to Know*. Boston: Houghton Mifflin.

Holland, Norman. 1975. *5 Readers Reading*. New Haven, CT: Yale University Press.

Holub, Robert C. 1984. *Reception Theory: A Critical Introduction*. New York: Methuen.

Iser, Wolfgang. 1978. *The Act of Reading: A Theory of Aesthetic Response*. Baltimore: Johns Hopkins University Press.

Jamie, Kathleen. 1987. "Grandmother's Ring." In: Angela Huth, ed. *Island of the Children: An Anthology of New Poems*. London: Orchard Books.

Jipson, Janice and Nicholas Paley. 1991. "The Selective Tradition in Teachers' Choice of Children's Literature: Does It Exist in the Elementary Classroom?" *English Education* 23(3): 148–59.

Johnson, Mark. 1987. *The Body in the Mind: The Bodily Basis of Meaning, Imagination, and Reason.* Chicago: University of Chicago Press.

Kasdorf, Julia. 1995. "First Gestures." *Poetry* 165(5): 261–62.

Kelly, George. 1955. *The Psychology of Personal Constructs.* Vols. 1 and 2. New York: Norton.

Lakoff, Robin Tolmach. 1990. *Talking Power: The Politics of Language in Our Lives.* New York: Basic Books.

Lancaster, Bruce. 1958. *The American Heritage Book of the Revolution.* New York: Simon & Schuster.

Leaper, Campbell. 1991. "Influence and Involvement in Children's Discourse: Age, Gender and Partner Effects." *Child Development* 62: 797–811.

Lee, Vernon. 1927/1968. *The Handling of Words and Other Studies in Literary Psychology.* Lincoln, NE: University of Nebraska Press.

Luke, Allan, Janine Cooke, and Carmen Luke. 1986. "The Selective Tradition in Action: Gender Bias in Student Teachers' Selections of Children's Literature." *English Education* 18(4): 209–18.

Mailloux, Steven. 1982. *Interpretive Conventions: The Reader in the Study of American Fiction.* Ithaca, NY: Cornell University Press.

Mailloux, Steven. 1990. "The Turns of Reader-Response Criticism." In: Charles Moran and Elizabeth F. Penfield, eds. *Conversations: Contemporary Critical Theory and the Teaching of Literature.* Urbana, IL: National Council of Teachers of English, 38–54.

Marshall, James. 1989. *Patterns of Discourse in Classroom Discussions of Literature.* Albany, NY: Center for the Learning and Teaching of Literature.

Martin, Bill. 1992. "Literature and Teaching: Getting Our Knowledge into Our Bones." *English Journal* 81(5): 56–60.

Meier, Daniel. 1 November 1987. "One Man's Kids." *New York Times,* section 6, p. 56.

Mellor, Bronwyn, Annette Patterson, and Marnie O'Neill. 1991. *Reading Fictions.* Scarborough, Australia: Chalkface Press.

Mill, John Stuart. 1859/1993. *On Liberty and Utilitarianism.* New York: Bantam Books.

Miller, Patrice, Dorothy Danaher, and David Forbes. 1986. "Sex-related Strategies for Coping with Interpersonal Conflict in Children Aged Five and Seven." *Developmental Psychology* 22: 543–48.

Milton, John. 1975. *The Christian Doctrine.* In: *Norton Critical Edition of Paradise Lost.* Scott Elledge, ed. New York: Norton.

Moon, Brian. 1990. *Studying Literature: Theory and Practice for Senior Students.* Scarborough, Australia: Chalkface Press.

Moran, Charles and Elizabeth F. Penfield, eds. *Conversations: Contemporary Critical Theory and the Teaching of Literature.* Urbana, IL: National Council of Teachers of English.

Morrison, Toni. 1987. In: William Zinsser, ed. *Inventing the Truth: The Art and Craft of Memoir.* Boston: Houghton Mifflin, 107–8.

Murfin, Ross C. 1993. "What Is Reader-Response Criticism?" In: James Joyce. *A Portrait of the Artist as a Young Man.* R. B. Kershner, ed. Boston: Bedford Books, 268–78.

Oates, Frederic J. 6 August 1989. "New Kid on Campus." *New York Times,* special section, Education Life, p. 58.

O'Hanlon, Christine. 1992. "Testing Out Developmental Psycholinguistics: Teachers Research the Adult/Child Role in Conversation." *English in Education* 26(1): 48–57.

Paley, Vivian Gussin. 1992. *You Can't Say You Can't Play.* Cambridge, MA: Harvard University Press.

Pradl, Gordon. 1991. "Reading in a Democracy: The Challenge of Louise Rosenblatt." In: John Clifford, ed. *The Experience of Reading: Louise Rosenblatt and Reader-Response Theory.* Portsmouth, NH: Boynton/Cook, 23–46.

Pradl, Gordon M. 1994. "Imagining Literature at the Point of Utterance." In: Bill Corcoran, Mike Hayhoe, and Gordon M. Pradl, eds. *Knowledge in the Making: Challenging the Text in the Classroom.* Portsmouth, NH: Heinemann, 233–44.

Probst, Robert E. 1988. "Dialogue with a Text." *English Journal* 77(1): 32–38.

Prose, Francine. 7 January 1990. "Confident at 11, Confused at 16." *New York Times,* section 6, pp. 22–25, 37–40, 45–46.

Ray, William. 1984. *Literary Meaning: From Phenomenology to Deconstruction.* Oxford: Basil Blackwell.

Roberts, Kenneth. 1940. *Oliver Wiswell.* New York: Doubleday, Doran & Co.

Rosenblatt, Louise. 1938. *Literature as Exploration.* New York: Appleton-Century-Crofts.

Rosenblatt, Louise. 1940. "Moderns Among Masterpieces." *English Leaflet* 39: 98–110.

Rosenblatt, Louise. 1964. "The Poem as Event." *College English* 26: 123–28.

Rosenblatt, Louise. 1968. *Literature as Exploration.* Rev. ed. New York: Noble and Noble.

Rosenblatt, Louise. 1978. *The Reader, the Text, the Poem: The Transactional Theory of the Literary Work.* Carbondale, IL: Southern Illinois University Press.

Rosenblatt, Louise. 1981. "The Reader's Contribution in the Literary Experience—Interview with Louise Rosenblatt." *The English Quarterly* XIV(1): 3–12.

Rosenblatt, Louise. 1990. "Retrospect." In: Edmund J. Farrell and James R. Squire, eds. *Transactions with Literature: A Fifty Year Perspective*. Urbana, IL: National Council of Teachers of English, 97–107.

Rothstein, Edward. 4 February 1991. "Roll Over Beethoven." *New Republic* 204(5): 29–34.

Rouse, John. 1978. *The Completed Gesture: Myth, Character and Education*. New Jersey: Skyline Books.

Sheldon, Amy. 1992. "Conflict Talk: Sociolinguistic Challenges to Self-assertion and How Young Girls Meet Them." *Merrill-Palmer Quarterly* 38: 95–117.

Smith, Barbara Herrnstein. 1988. *Contingencies of Value: Alternative Perspectives for Critical Theory*. Cambridge, MA: Harvard University Press.

Sommers, Nancy. 1993. "I Stand Here Writing." *College English* 55(4): 420–28.

Stillman, Peter R. 1993. "Coming Down the Kuskokwim." *College English* 55(2): 208–9.

Stotsky, Sandra. 1991. *Connecting Civic Education & Language Education: The Contemporary Challenge*. New York: Teachers College Press.

Tannen, Deborah. 1990. *You Just Don't Understand: Women and Men in Conversation*. New York: William Morrow.

Tarde, Gabriel. 1969. *On Communication and Social Influence: Selected Papers*. Terry N. Clark, ed. Chicago: University of Chicago Press.

Thomas, R. S. 1990. *Counterpoint*. Newcastle upon Tyne, England: Bloodaxe Books.

Tompkins, Jane P., ed. 1980. *Reader Response Criticism: From Formalism to Post-Structuralism*. Baltimore: Johns Hopkins University Press.

Wertheimer, Max. 1959. *Productive Thinking*. Enlarged edition. New York: Harper & Row.

Wieland, Sharon. 1990. "Leading Classroom Discussions." *CSSEDC Quarterly* 12(4): 1–3.

Wood, Gordon. 1991. *The Radicalism of the American Revolution*. New York: Knopf.

INDEX

Access, 5, 11, 42, 51, 81, 107, 108, 135, 137, 144, 151
Adams, John, 6
Agency, 1, 9, 34, 55, 71, 81, 124, 125, 132, 144
    student, 34–39
Alienation, 17, 77, 86, 87, 100, 123, 150
Allen, Gracie, 13
Ambiguity, 17, 22, 40, 46, 58, 62, 106, 127, 148, 150, 152
American Revolution, 58–65
Animal Farm, 132
Arnold, Benedict, 62
Auerbach, Red, 32
Austen, Jane, 70
Authority, 1, 8, 11, 16, 19, 22, 26, 27, 31–33, 45, 48, 56, 67, 75, 86, 132
    as a middle-class anxiety, 39–40
    challenging, 23–26, 137
    contesting, 34–35
    crisis of, 16–17, 152
    decline of, 42, 50
    overthrowing, 38–39
    questioning, 36–38, 49
    relinquishing, 50
    resisting, 35–36
    sharing, 50
    sources of, 15–17, 41, 49–50
    traditional patterns of, 68, 72
Autonomy, 4, 71, 118, 152

Barrymore, John, 32
Barthes, Roland, 72

Belief, 16, 22, 24, 64, 147, 149
Bentley, Arthur, 84
Berlin, Isaiah, 148
Berryman, John, 32
Bleich, David, 83, 88
Bloom, Harold, 29
Boethius, 131
Booth, Wayne, 84, 93
Britton, James, 53
Brown, Lyn Mikel
    Meeting at the Crossroads, 53–56
Bruner, Jerome, 8
Burke, Kenneth, 83
Burnheim, John, 8, 42

Canon, 9, 14, 85, 103, 135
Canterford, Barbara, 68
Catton, Bruce, 59–60
Certainty, 1, 5, 8, 104, 107, 108, 149
Change, 1, 6, 7, 8, 13, 26, 33, 37, 70, 85, 90, 95, 99, 105, 116, 128, 129, 139, 142, 147
Cherryholmes, Cleo, 103
Christian-Smith, Linda, 86
Clarke, Dr. John, 64
Closure, 48, 95, 107, 143, 151
Collaboration, 9, 25, 40, 79, 83, 88, 89, 98, 101, 108, 110, 130, 151, 152
Collins, Jackie, 133
Commitment, 8, 15, 45, 47, 57, 108, 119, 147, 148, 150
Community, 14, 19, 21, 22, 47, 55, 77, 81, 97, 100, 101, 107, 108, 136, 146–147

Competition, 7, 29, 47, 55, 100,
    103, 105, 150
Confidence, 9, 11, 19, 26, 27, 29, 32,
    52, 70, 72, 77, 105, 108, 110,
    130, 131, 138, 146, 147, 152
Constructive thinking, 89–92
Constructivism, social, 8, 24–26,
    27, 47, 86, 88, 90, 102, 152
Constructs, personal, 69–70
Context, 29, 31–32, 51, 74, 75, 79,
    82, 149
Control, 5, 14, 16, 37, 41, 46, 47, 68,
    70, 90, 92, 94, 101, 103, 106,
    107, 109, 110, 128, 131, 151
Conversation, 7, 10, 11, 14, 15, 16,
    21, 32, 35, 36, 37, 47, 52, 53,
    54, 58, 67, 68, 71, 74, 77, 83,
    88, 94–106, 108, 110, 117,
    127, 130–134, 136, 144–152
    reading, 134, 137–138
    written, 110–119, 120–127
Cooperation, 7, 108
Culler, Jonathan, 83
Cultural critics, 85–87
Cultural pluralism, 135–137
Culture wars, 26

Danish, Barbara, 104
Davidson, Peter, 32
Davies, Robertson, 47
Democracy, 1, 4–11, 23, 36, 41–42,
    46, 51, 58, 68, 72, 74–77, 81–
    83, 86–89, 92, 98, 99, 102,
    106, 107, 110, 122, 128–130,
    132, 135, 136, 138, 143, 144,
    146–152
Derrida, Jacques, 30
Dewey, John, 7, 76, 83, 84, 90–91,
    107, 147
Dialogue, 7, 9, 31, 70, 75, 78, 82,
    95, 102, 104, 105, 128, 132,
    134, 136, 141
Dias, Patrick, 89, 119
Difference, 6, 26, 41–42, 45, 54, 62,
    77, 88, 95, 132, 135, 137, 144,
    147–149, 152
Disagreement, 10, 16, 35, 80, 94,

    95, 101, 108, 124, 130, 132,
    133, 150
Discourse of certainty, 104
Discourse of possibility, 104–105
Discrepancy, 18, 19, 58, 105, 131
Discussion, 10, 35, 36, 38, 75, 103,
    109, 110, 111, 113, 114, 115,
    117, 118, 130, 138
Dominance, 1, 101, 107, 149
Donaldson, Margaret, 59

Ehrenreich, Barbara, 39–40
Elites, 4–6, 135, 144
Ellenport, Sam, 96
Emig, Janet, 85
Emotion, 15, 19, 32, 45, 52, 56, 61,
    82, 90–92, 102, 113, 116, 117,
    139, 140, 141
Evidence, 27, 104, 129
Exclusion, 6, 21, 41–46, 65, 136
Experience, 15, 16, 18, 19, 23–25,
    29, 31, 76, 77, 82, 89, 106,
    122, 125, 129, 130, 132, 133,
    134, 137, 143, 147, 149, 152
    of words in the body, 51–53
Experimental method, 7

Fairness, 17, 42, 43, 44, 55, 136, 149
Faulkner, William
    Sound and the Fury, The, 144
Fish, Stanley, 83
Foundationalism, 84
Frank, Anne, 55
Franklin, Benjamin, 62
Frost, Robert, 89
Fry, Donald, 138

Gender, 7, 28, 49, 53–57, 85, 86, 99–
    102, 124, 125, 127, 128, 150
Gere, Anne Ruggles, 87–88
Gilligan, Carol, 55, 100
    Meeting at the Crossroads, 53–
    56
Ginsberg, Alan, 135
Gone with the Wind, 125
Greider, William, 147
Gulliver's Travels, 144

Hamilton, Alexander 6
Hawthorne, Nathaniel, 17–18
    "Young Goodman Brown",
    17–22, 24
Hierarchy, 1, 4–7, 8, 9, 11, 28, 40,
    41, 44, 46, 51, 74, 81, 97,
    100, 101, 103, 135, 150, 152
Hirsch, E. D., 29, 135
Holland, Norman, 31, 78, 82, 83, 88
Holub, Robert, 83
*Huckleberry Finn, The Adventures
    of*, 129
Husserl, Edmund, 83
Hypocrisy, 17

Identity, 9, 13, 16, 27, 48, 63, 68
Imagination, 10, 45, 47, 50, 52, 58,
    62, 92, 94, 105, 122, 147,
    152
Imposition, 97, 134
Inclusion, 47, 57, 98, 107
Indeterminacy, 15, 31, 106, 107,
    110, 152
Individual, 1, 6, 7, 11, 22, 39, 65,
    72, 74, 75, 77, 79, 81, 82, 83,
    86, 88, 92, 98, 110, 132,
    150–152
Information explosion, 135
Innocence, loss of, 18, 19, 22
Innovation, 48, 147
Intertextuality, 29, 134
Invention, 10, 36, 96, 98, 150
Ironic involvement, 17, 46–48, 50,
    147–148
Iser, Wolfgang, 83

James, William, 83
Jamie, Kathleen, 111
Jay, John, 60
Jefferson, Thomas, 6
Jipson, Janice, 136
Joel, Billy, 135
Johnson, Mark, 51
Joyce, James, 85

Kasdorf, Julia, 121, 127–128
Kelly, George, 24, 69–70

Lafayette, Marquis de, 62
Lakoff, Robin, 101
Leaper, Campbell, 101
Lee, Vernon, 84
Listening, 4, 11, 34, 37, 51–57, 74,
    88, 92, 94, 99, 100, 103, 109,
    147
    role of constructs in, 69–70
    teacher and, 66–73, 146
Literature, 15, 25, 45, 50–51, 65,
    74–80, 102–106, 108, 132,
    133, 138, 143, 149–152
Lodge, David, 29
Lorenzo's Oil, 142–143
Lowell, Robert, 126
Luke, Allan, 136

Madison, James, 6
Magorian, Michelle, 139–141
Mailloux, Steven, 83–85, 129
Marshall, James, 103
Marvell, Andrew, 56
Mature dependency, 71–72
Maturity, 17, 19, 50, 72, 91, 116
McLean, Don, 135
Meaning, 14, 26, 79, 82, 88, 99, 110,
    113, 127, 128, 129, 150–152
Mediate, mediation, 3, 4, 6, 7, 9,
    19, 24, 47, 61, 77, 80, 94, 106,
    107, 125
Meier, Daniel, 102
Mellor, Bronwyn, 86
Mill, John Stuart, 149
Miller, Patrice, 101
Milton, John, 20
Monologue, 11, 75, 96
Moon, Brian, 86
Morrison, Toni, 10, 30
Motives, 15, 19, 21, 25, 59, 76, 103,
    147
Multiculturalism, 136, 148
Museum of Bad Art, 31
Mutual, mutuality, 5, 7, 9, 20, 52,
    68, 70, 99, 103, 104, 106, 107,
    129, 149
Myth, 20, 21, 23, 24–25, 26, 27, 31,
    32, 43, 45, 59

Myth-Making, 23, 25, 26

Narrative, 1, 9, 10, 25, 64, 65, 70, 101, 124, 125, 127, 128, 144
National Oracy Project, 73
Negotiation, 4, 6, 7, 10, 22, 52, 61, 96, 105, 106, 107, 108, 110, 118, 119, 124, 136, 146, 150, 151, 152
Nolte, Nick, 142
Novelty, 8, 27, 107

Oakeshott, Michael, 97–98
Oates, Frederic, 143–145
Oates, Joyce Carol, 144
O'Hanlon, Christine, 66–67
Opposites, 24–25, 47, 101
Other Way to Listen, The, 68
Ownership, 16, 50, 132

Paley, Nicholas, 136
Paley, Vivian Gussin, 42–46, 47
Performing the literary text, 110
Perspective, 1, 3, 4, 5, 7, 8, 10, 11, 16, 17, 21, 24, 27, 34, 45, 48, 49, 58, 59, 60, 62, 63, 64, 70, 77, 94, 95, 105–108, 117, 123, 129, 133–137, 146, 152
Plato, 4
Play, 7, 14, 27, 37, 43–44, 45, 47, 56, 72, 79, 96, 106, 108, 114, 122, 125
Pluralism, 11, 27, 40, 59, 65, 106, 133, 135–137, 148
Possibility, 1, 11, 104–105, 146–152
Poststructuralism, 85, 107, 148
Power, 4–5, 10, 14, 40, 41, 44, 47, 55, 68, 72, 78, 86, 97, 103, 116, 123, 124, 125, 136, 139, 151, 152
Pradl, Gordon, 33, 80
Pragmatism, 84
Prejudice, 23, 70, 90, 104, 135, 142, 147, 148
Printing press, 132

Privilege, 4–6, 7, 14, 26, 40, 41–50, 65, 99, 135, 137
Probst, Robert, 89

Ray, William, 83
Reader response, 29, 75, 78–79, 81–89, 92, 107, 141
Reading
  dominating, 28–33
  histories, 137–142, 143–145
  mishaps, 142–143
  open acts of, 26–28, 74, 112
  pleasure, 23, 29–30, 46–48, 108, 132, 133, 144
  primary acts of, 31–32, 33
  resistant, 56
  responsible, 30
  secondary acts of, 33
  social act, as a, 4, 10, 11, 51, 102, 107, 127, 129, 130, 132, 141, 149, 150
  temporal aspect of, 128–129, 137–143
Reason, 89–93, 97, 104, 105
Reception theory, 29, 83
Reciprocity, 6, 7, 47, 70, 72, 99, 103, 146, 152
Reilly, Jerry, 31
Relationship, 1, 4, 7, 8, 9, 11, 16, 43, 51, 53, 55, 69, 74, 86, 87, 90, 95, 96, 100, 101, 103, 106, 112–114, 117, 123, 130, 146, 147, 149–152
  book-owner, 131–132
  caring, 47
  horizontal, 31
  knower-known, 71, 84
  power, 68
  reader-author, 28
  reader-teacher, 28
  reader-text, 75, 78–79
  teacher-learner, 25, 36
  teacher-student, 151
  vertical, 31, 41
Relativity, 25, 28, 40, 47, 49, 79, 148
Resistance, 27, 56, 70

Responsibility, 4, 8, 9, 14, 17, 34, 36, 37, 40, 46, 72, 76, 78, 95, 107, 123, 152
Robert's Rules, 96–97
Roberts, Kenneth
    Oliver Wiswell, 60–63
Rosenblatt, Louise, 74–80, 81–93, 128
    Literature as Exploration, 75–78, 87, 89–93
    "Poem as Event, The", 83
Rothstein, Edward, 148
Rouse, John, 23–26
Rover Boys, The, 144

Sacks, Oliver, 80
Santayana, George, 5
Sarandon, Susan, 142
Scientific method, 135
Selective tradition, 136
Self-expression, 9, 52, 53
Shanker, Albert, 96
Sheldon, Amy, 102
Slave narratives, 10
Small groups, 117–119, 129–130
Smith, Barbara Herrnstein, 49
Smith, Jenifer, 111
Social determinism, 77
Sommers, Nancy 35
Speech acts, 101
Spragg, Captain Thomas, 63–64
Standards, 5, 25, 50, 55, 135, 136
Status, 4, 14, 39, 41–50, 99, 103
Stillman, Peter, 2–4, 11
    "Coming Down the Kuskokwim", 2–4, 11, 152
Story, 7, 16, 19, 21, 24, 27, 38, 45, 46, 48, 50, 52, 72, 73, 112, 113, 114, 124, 128, 144, 146
Stotsky, Sandra, 95
Subordination, 5, 99, 134

Tannen, Deborah, 99
Tarde, Gabriel, 98–99
Thomas, R. S., 118
To Kill a Mockingbird, 133
Tocqueville, Alexis de, 77, 132, 150
Tolerance, 4, 40, 106, 127, 133, 139, 147–150
Tom Sawyer, 144
Tom Swift, 144
Tompkins, Jane, 81–82
Transaction, transactional, 7, 24, 26, 75–80, 81, 84, 88–89, 92, 95, 108, 150
Transformation, 1, 5, 7, 10, 55, 81, 87, 103
Transmission, 15, 24, 25, 27, 28, 106
Trashy books, 133
Trust, 47, 70, 92, 94, 95, 108, 137, 152

Uncertainty, 15, 17, 54, 90, 92, 107, 108, 110, 111, 127, 147–150, 152
United Empire Loyalists, 61

Values, 4, 8, 11, 19, 25, 27, 43, 75, 78, 86, 103, 108, 148
Voluntarism, 77
Vulnerability, 34, 44, 48–50, 52, 92, 95, 107, 125, 130, 152

Washington, George, 62
Weber, Julia, 146–147
Wertheimer, Max, 69
Wieland, Sharon, 68
Winnicott, Donald, 79
Wisdom, wise, 4, 5, 28, 29, 108, 126
Wood, Gordon, 5

Yeats, W. B.,
    "The Wild Swans at Coole", 2